Throwing the Stick Forward

African Women for Peace Series

Somalia between peace and war: Somali women on the eve of
the 21st century

Sudan between peace and war: internally displaced women in
Khartoum and South and West Kordofan

Engendering peace: reflections on the Burundi peace process

Throwing the stick forward: the impact of war on southern
Sudanese women

Throwing the Stick Forward
the impact of war on southern Sudanese women

Mary Anne Fitzgerald

African Women for Peace Series

UNIFEM & UNICEF

This publication has been supported by the financial contribution of the Royal Netherlands Embassy in Nairobi Kenya.

this book is published by
United Nations Development Fund for Women (UNIFEM)
PO Box 30218, Nairobi, Kenya
Web site: http://www.unifem.undp.org
&
United Nations Children's Fund
PO Box 44145, Nairobi, Kenya
Website: http://www.unicef.org

UNIFEM is the women's fund at the United Nations. It provides financial and technical assistance to innovative programmes and strategies that promote women's human rights, political participation and economic security. UNIFEM works in partnership with UN organizations, governments, and non-governmental organizations (NGOs) and networks to promote gender equality. It links women's issues and concerns to national, regional and global agendas, by fostering collaboration and providing technical expertise on how to place gender in the mainstream and empower women.

UNICEF is mandated by the United Nations General Assembly to advocate the protection of children's rights, to help meet their basic needs and to expand their opportunities to reach their full potential. UNICEF aims, through its country programmes, to promote the equal rights of women and girls and to support their full participation in the political, social and economic development of their communities.

ISBN 9966-950-24-9

edited by Helen van Houten
design and layout by Michelle Mathews
cover photo by Betty Press
this publication has been coordinated by Hodan Addou and Julianna Lindsey
scanning by InCA
films by Marketpower Int
printed by Kenya Litho

contents

abbreviations and definitions

IDP	internally displaced person
IGAD	Inter-Governmental Authority on Development
IRIN	Integrated Regional Information Network, United Nations Office for the Coordination of Humanitarian Affairs
KES	Kenya shilling, valued at 78 to USD 1 in 2002
NGO	non-governmental organization
NSCC	New Sudan Council of Churches
NSWF	New Sudan Women's Federation
OLS	Operation Lifeline Sudan
PTSD	post-traumatic stress disorder
RASS	Relief Association of Southern Sudan
SPDF	Sudan People's Democratic Front
SPLA	Sudanese People's Liberation Army
SRRA	Sudan Relief and Rehabilitation Association
SSLM	South Sudan Liberation Movement
SWAN	Sudanese Women's Association in Nairobi
SWNP	Sudanese Women's Voice for Peace
UNICEF	United Nations Children's Fund
UNIFEM	United Nations Development Fund for Women
USD	United States dollar
WFP	World Food Programme
WODRANS	Widows, Orphans and the Disabled Rehabilitation Association of the New Sudan
bridewealth	the amount a groom or his family gives to the bride's family
murahaleen	nomadic militias
payam	district
tukul	round hut

preface

This book is a rare opportunity for the voices to be heard of the women who have borne the brunt of one of the most brutal wars of our time. Among the different ethnic groups of southern Sudan it is the women who never shirk community responsibilities just as they continue to fetch firewood, till the soil and nurse their young no matter what is happening around them. This burden, carried in a silence enforced by convention, has been made infinitely worse by a 20-year-old civil war that has provoked regular famine and taken the lives of a disproportionate number of women and children.

This book is not about people waiting for help to arrive. It is an inspiring insight into the lives of women who have become peacemakers and leaders despite having to put their energies into simple survival day after day. That such women can emerge from the rapes, abductions and atrocities of this horrific conflict determined to take on higher challenges says much for their inner strength and resilience. It is our hope that more of this latent potential among the women and girls of southern Sudan can be realized.

I would like to thank all the women in southern Sudan who gave freely and generously of their time to answer endless questions. I am particularly grateful for the trust they showed me by sharing personal confidences and retelling painful experiences. Very special thanks go to the women at Kakuma refugee camp, who have endured so much in silence. Their courage and fortitude are humbling.

Some of the people named here gave interviews; others took the time to consider and debate several aspects of the manuscript. The list is long: Sitouna Abdallah, Adam Abdelmoula, Intisar Abdel-Sadiq, Anisia Achieng, Alberto Carlos Cabeia Chys, Awut

Deng, Laketch Dirasse, Paula Donovan, Hamid El-Bashir, Marguerite Garling, Rebecca Okwaci Joshua, Jennifer Klot, Keziah (Mama) Layinwa Nicodemus, Mary Naulang, Nadi Osodo, Hendrica Okondo, Pauline Riak, Christine Sadia, Joanne Sandler, Sihaka Tsemo.

I hope that the contribution these women and men have made to this book will help to enlighten the world about the daily struggles of the women of southern Sudan and will bear fruit through better-informed projects, more thoughtful assistance and lasting peace for them.

Mary Anne Fitzgerald

introduction

*I ask you this. Since the creation of earth, in all of human history, has
any man ever died with a child in his womb? We women alone know the
pain of giving birth. Our words and our thoughts must be taken
seriously. If you don't, then you must understand that we women will
make a revolution. We will stop giving birth.*

Debora Nyandien, delegate to the West Bank Peace Council

Southern Sudan's women suffer some of the poorest quality of
life indices in the world. The 865 maternal deaths for every
100,000 live births that occur in some of the war-affected areas is
appalling. One doctor for every 222,000 people could hardly be
worse. A 90% illiteracy rate among adult women is not only
woeful but discriminatory. These statistics make the point
vividly—war is destructive.[1]

Women could be a positive force for improvement, but they
face many obstacles. They are weakened by anaemia. They cannot
do sums. They lack self-esteem. This would not be so if they
enjoyed equal access to resources such as health, education and
agriculture. There is cultural bias against their participation in
community projects. They are also traumatized by violence and
enjoy little legal protection. They have little time to change any of
this, even if they could, because they routinely work up to 17 hours
a day.

The purpose of this book is not to underscore the litany of
woes that beset the women of southern Sudan but to find a way
forward within the context of their culture and circumstances. Aid
workers cannot be part of this process without understanding and
respecting the women's perspective on life. This is why the
following chapters not only outline the problems Sudanese
women confront on a daily basis but also provide a stage from

1

which their voices can be heard. Listening to the women articulate their needs is the starting point from which to look for solutions.

background

2

To understand the impact of the war on women we need to understand the political history of Sudan and the genesis of the long civil war.

For the best part of 50 years peace has eluded the peoples of southern Sudan. The reason is rooted in a long-standing rebellion of the Nilotic and Bantu southerners against the arabized government of the north. However, the conflict is far more complex and chaotic than a mere civil war. It has been intensified by fierce interethnic rivalries among the southerners, which have pitted opposition fighting forces against each other. In addition, some of the southern rebels are allied with a coalition of northern opposition political parties to engage government forces in battle along the combat line between north and south. Fighting is characterized by regular attacks and atrocities of one military or ethnic faction against another interspersed with fierce military battles. The fighting continues to the present day. The current round of civil war has killed more people than in Kosovo, Bosnia, Rwanda and Somalia combined, most of them civilians. The population in the south is declining at an annual rate of 1.9% compared with a growth of 2.9% in the rest of Sudan.[2] To understand the war's genesis, one must look at the history of Sudan.

Sudan is the ninth largest country in the world and Africa's largest. Its 2.5 million square kilometres stretch from the tropical forests, mountains and savannahs of the south to the arid Sahel belt in the north. The vastness and the complexity that characterize this geography are reflected in Sudan's peoples. There are some 570 different ethnic groups, of which nearly 40% are native Arabic speakers who live in northern and central Sudan. The great majority of Bantu and Nilotic Sudanese live in the

3

south. Many of the Bantu peoples, such as the Azande, live along Sudan's southern borders, and many of the semi-nomadic Nilotes, such as the Dinka, Nuer and Shilluk, occupy the central and northern expanses of southern Sudan. There are approximately 5 million Christians among a total population of 35 million,[3] although a census has not been conducted for many years. The ethnic divide between north and south is accentuated by the distinct variance of geography, political ambitions, religion and rate of development.

Southern Sudan accounts for almost one-third of the country. It is so large that it is equivalent to the landmass of Burundi, Kenya, Rwanda, Tanzania and Uganda combined. Its natural resources include oil, water, timber and unexploited fertile land. It is bisected on a north–south axis by the White Nile as it flows north to join the Blue Nile at Khartoum. Between Bor and Adok the river spills over hundreds of square kilometres to form the Sudd, which is the largest swamp in the world. This untouched watery wilderness that expands and contracts seasonally is negotiated only by dugout canoes and barges travelling the Nile. It has effectively provided a barrier—which is what the word 'sudd' means—preventing outsiders from penetrating it. The Sudd is one of the reasons why southern Sudan has been neglected in terms of development. And since the onset of the war, what little infrastructure that existed either has been destroyed or has fallen into disrepair.

Northern Sudan's written history dates back thousands of years to the Cush kingdom of the Old Testament. Islam became the dominant religion of northern Sudan during the Islamic conquest in the 13th century. It was ruled from the Ottoman Empire for several centuries. In 1821, the viceroy of Egypt, Muhammad Ali, conquered northern Sudan and opened up trade routes through the Sudd to the previously isolated south. After this, Sudanese Arab commerce with Egyptians and Europeans was

4

expanded to include the export of ivory and slaves. Over the next decades the southern population of Nilotes and Bantu peoples was substantially reduced through pillage, slaving raids and disease. Expeditions to the south were carried out under an Egyptian flag, but they increasingly involved the British, who were seeking a foothold in Central Africa. As far as the outside world was concerned, this vast area was the dominion of Arab slavers, European explorers and the occasional outpost garrison of Egyptian soldiers.

Towards the end of the 19th century northern Sudan entered a period of bloody confrontation between the Mahdist movement of ascetic Muslims and the Egyptians and British. The British strategy to separate Sudan from Egypt and integrate southern Sudan into a British East Africa federation was a failure that culminated in the Mahdi's successful siege of Khartoum and the murder of General Gordon. Then in 1898 Anglo-Egyptian troops under the command of Lord Kitchener defeated the Mahdists at Omdurman, and the British signed a condominium agreement with Egypt that effectively accorded the British political domination. For nearly 60 years, the British held sway over a region that stretched from the Egyptian border in the north to Kenya, Uganda and what is now the Democratic Republic of the Congo in the south. Southern administrative outposts created a handful of towns such as Juba, Malakal, Wau, Yambio and Yei. However, long distances and poor transport systems meant that communications with the seat of government in Khartoum were patchy at best. The vast majority of southerners remained beyond the writ of authority and the reach of progress.

The British created a fledgling state in the staunchly Islamic Arab north with an infrastructure of roads, railways, irrigation works, ports and civil service that was based on an export economy of gum arabic and cotton. While this was happening, the Mahdi's family, by now a semi-feudal aristocracy that enjoyed a ground swell of support, was advocating independence from Egypt. Fearing nationwide rebellion, the British isolated the south by making it a 'closed district'. Some British administrators also harboured the idea that the 'African' south should be hived off to become part of East Africa. This in turn may have stalled much of the progress that might have come the southerners' way. They were largely excluded from development and received few of the economic benefits that the northern part of the country enjoyed, a trend that pertains even today.

The decision to forestall regional integration accentuated the disparity of economies and religious and cultural beliefs between north and south, which was to have profound long-term implications for Sudan's future. Southern religion is rooted in ancestor worship with an overlay of missionary Christianity. Only about one in five southern Sudanese is Christian, but because of their education, their influence is strong. Bantu and Nilotic societies acknowledge authority in the form of chiefs among peers. After independence, this was exploited to co-opt tribal leaders and educated Christians as petty functionaries while arabized northerners held most of the positions of authority. Southerners continue to subsist on an introverted economy of small-scale agriculture, fishing and cattle.

Southern rebellion began to simmer when demands for either secession or a federal government were ignored. At independence on 1 January 1956, the region was in the throes of a full-scale civil war. By 1963 the army's Equatoria Corps had mutinied to form the backbone of the Anyanya ('snake poison') secessionist movement. In the north, the Mahdi's great grandson Sadiq al-Mahdi succeeded the founding administration of General Ibrahim Abboud only to be overthrown in 1969 by Jafaar el-Nimeiry's military coup supported by the Communist party. Nimeiry brought an interregnum of peace to the south in 1972 with the Addis Ababa Accord that allowed for limited autonomy through the Southern Regional Assembly, which was seated in the southern capital of Juba.

A Nimeiry colleague, Abel Alier, a Bor Dinka, served as president of the High Executive Council of the Southern Region from 1972 to 1982 with the exception of some months in 1978 and 1979 when the post was held by Joseph Lagu, a Madi. On Lagu's resignation, he campaigned to subdivide the south into three semi-autonomous regions on the grounds that this would allay Dinka dominance of southern politics. Lagu's detractors, who felt this fragmentation would diminish their bargaining power with the Khartoum government, formed an opposition Council for the Unity of Southern Sudan. Even though they won the majority of seats in the Regional Assembly's 1982 elections, Nimeiry appointed James Tombura, a pro-divisionist, as president of the region. The division issue fractured southern unity as well as widened the north–south rift.

Relations deteriorated further over plans to build the Jonglei Canal and to drill for oil in Western Upper Nile, projects whose benefits would bypass the south. The proposed 200-mile canal was designed to divert the White Nile around the Sudd in order to increase the water supply to northern Sudan and Egypt. Based on the discovery of commercial quantities of oil by the US firm Chevron some 800 kilometres south-west of Khartoum near Bentiu, Nimeiry announced a massive exploration programme covering 550,000 square kilometres. The plan was to export the extracted oil by piping it directly to a terminal near Port Sudan.

Both projects were abandoned in the wake of renewed fighting.* In March 1983, Nimeiry called in ex-Anyanya fighter Colonel John Garang to quash a mutiny of his troops. The ploy

---

* The Jonglei Canal project was abandoned when the local tribes, who resented it, effectively stopped the work by holding 10 French workers hostage.

backfired. Garang, a Bor Dinka from Jonglei who had attended staff college in the United States, encouraged defections from southern garrisons. Southern troops objected to the Khartoum policy of gutting the south of its fighters by redeploying them in the north. By September of that year, Garang had mustered a 6,000-strong Sudanese People's Liberation Army (SPLA). Nimeiry was overthrown in 1985 and replaced by a shaky coalition government headed by Sadiq al-Mahdi. Four years on, General Omar Hassan Ahmed El-Beshir seized control in a bloodless coup. Beshir's military regime continues to govern Sudan through the Revolutionary Command Council for National Salvation.

At the time of its inception, the SPLA opposed Nimeiry's policies of arabization of the south including the imposition of Islamic sharia law on non-Muslim peoples. Today Garang's stated objective of the SPLA for the people of southern Sudan is a confederation linking a secular state in the south to an Islamic state in the north with an eventual referendum on self-determination.

Headed by Garang, the SPLA controls most of Eastern and Western Equatoria, Bahr el Ghazal and Lakes. The government retains hold of several towns including Juba, Kapoeta and Torit in Equatoria, Bor in Jonglei, Aweil and Wau in Bahr el Ghazal, and Malakal in Upper Nile.

The exploration and extraction of commercial quantities of oil in the south is a major cause of the continued prosecution of the civil war and the direct cause for the catastrophic disruption of the lives of the Nuer people who live in oil production and exploration areas.[4] According to the UN Special Rapporteur to Sudan, Gerhard Baum, it 'has led to a worsening of the conflict, which has also turned into a war for oil. . . . There is no concrete evidence of oil revenues being spent for the development of the south, in spite of the fact that 40% of the national budget comes from oil,' he added.[5] In the 1980s the Nuer and Dinka who were native to the area surrounding the Unity and Heglig oilfields were permanently displaced.[6] The re-entry of foreign-led oil consortiums in the 1990s coincided with a resurgence of atrocities that has 'created a swath of scorched earth' around the oil fields.[7] Tens of thousands of people have been forced to leave their homes since 1999 through tactics such as ground attacks, strafing from helicopter gunships and aerial bombardments.[8] At Adar Yel in Eastern Upper Nile, where an oil consortium began prospecting in March 2001, 48 villages were burned and 55,000 people displaced to clear the area of potential 'insurgents'.[9] Reported human rights abuses include mass executions of male villagers and the nailing of women and children to trees with iron spikes.[10]

Government bombing of civilian targets such as hospitals, schools, relief centres and market places intensified during 2000. Shifting alliances and power strategies of the military leaders of local tribal factions have created further disruptions. Traditional rivalry among different southern ethnic groups has in the past contributed significantly to unrest in rebel areas. The alliances of local military leaders shift like a kaleidoscope, and to be efficient and safe, anyone working in southern Sudan must be aware of local politics. Local political affiliations are influenced by the chance for power, territorial gain and access to arms and military hardware. As with the existence of commercial quantities of high-grade oil, these conflict constituencies have undermined efforts to achieve peace. It has been estimated that over the last few years the death toll from interfactional fighting has exceeded that from encounters with government forces.[11] In a significant step towards southern unity, Dr Riek Machar's Sudan People's Democratic Front (SPDF) merged with the SPLA in January 2002. The most notable of the splinter rebel factions, the SPDF comprised a Nuer following. The following month government bombing of civilian targets, particularly relief centres, intensified.[12]

The resulting disruption in the lives of the southerners has been massive and catastrophic. The latest round of civil war has claimed around 2 million lives. More than 4.5 million have been displaced, often several times and sometimes for more than 15 years. More than one million live in exile, the great majority as refugees in neighbouring countries.[13]

Little activity from the international community occurred in southern Sudan until the UN's Operation Lifeline Sudan (OLS) started in 1989 as a means to negotiate access to areas of fighting. Originally conceived in the wake of the severe 1988 famine as a short-term supply line for relief food, its mandate for southern Sudan has been extended to become a consortium of United Nations agencies and international NGOs conducting humanitarian intervention to all civilians in need, regardless of their location or factional affiliation. OLS is operated under a tripartite agreement with the government of Sudan, the SPLM and UNICEF, which represents the United Nations. It operates from bases in Khartoum and Lokichoggio, a small Kenyan town near the Sudan border. The ground rules developed in the mid-1990s require the agencies and the warring parties in rebel areas to respect international humanitarian law. Minimum operating standards, which are separate from the ground rules, allow for the negotiation of security and access by rail and roads that cross the lines between the warring parties. In 1998 the obligations and expectations relevant to these corridors of access were discussed among the Technical Committee for Humanitarian Assistance, which includes the Sudanese government and the SPLM, but an agreement has yet to be ratified. Since the inception of OLS, the government has imposed arbitrary flight bans, which often hamper distribution of aid to southerners whose survival is precarious. Some international NGOs operate outside the OLS umbrella, preferring to work solely with the SPLM or other factions.

Women and children in southern Sudan suffer the combined

impact of underdevelopment and war more than any other segment of the population. Eighty per cent of all war-related deaths have been unarmed civilians, and most of these casualties were women and children.[14] However, despite the dire circumstances in which they are living, these women and children are dreaming of a homeland that is peaceful—one in which girls have access to education and where the women can engage in business ventures. It is their hope that through cooperation and hard work, they can pool what resources they have to turn this dream into reality.

women's status in society 3

atnel ci biok tneng – throwing the stick forward

The disruption of traditional social systems through conflict and natural disaster, displacement and famine has plunged the status of the contemporary southern Sudanese woman into a state of flux. The cultural frame within which she operates, dependent on kinship ties within lineal groups, ceases to function normally when family and clan members are dispersed and resources have become scarce. Property and livestock loss incurred through war, and crop failure as a result of drought, flood and population displacement have served to impoverish the southern Sudanese. This rift in the historical status quo has accentuated the fundamental, traditional imbalance between men and women. Women have become more impoverished than men.

This has proved to be a mixed blessing. As is often the case with violent social upheaval, fractured lives can present cracks of opportunity for constructive change. A woman may be homeless, hungry and frightened, but at the same time she is liberated from traditional constraints. In the vacuum created by the disintegration of the clan support system, she has discovered the licence to implement innovative survival strategies that transcend the traditional gender roles.

In other words, the war has instigated the breakdown of traditional barriers, saddling women with additional responsibilities but also offering them the chance to throw off old prohibitions and constraints. Left to fend for themselves any way they can, women are newly acquiring knowledge and skills that, in turn, are reshaping gender roles and kinship dependency.

Families are scattered by the centrifugal forces of fighting and famine. When this occurs, the men revert to their roles of

12

breadwinners, guardians and warriors even though their motives are not always fired with altruism. In times of economic hardship they might head to northern Sudan in search of work, leaving the family behind in the south. Then famine or fighting occurs, and the women and children migrate in search of sustenance and sanctuary to a feeding centre, a camp for displaced people inside Sudan or a refugee camp outside the country. Sometimes men chaperone their families on the trek to these places. Then they return to look after the family assets—the cattle herds or the fields—or to enlist in the military or return to the front. If resources are scarce and there is not enough food to go around, they might dispatch some of their wives to a feeding centre or refugee camp and retain others by their side at home. They could then alternate between the two sets of families, visiting one before returning home to the other. The permutations of migration are complex and unpredictable.

Only a third of the adult population is male. In Bahr el Ghazal where conflict is most frequent, the percentage shrinks to 25%.[15] Men are either under arms, have been killed in battle, or have left the south for training or in search of money. A woman whose husband is absent or dead discovers she is capable of performing his tasks around the compound. As she is now responsible for the children, she seeks to replace his income-earning ability by learning his skills. And in so doing, she cries out to be literate and numerate. The woman who launches on this trajectory of education and self reliance has begun to assert her basic human rights. Once this happens, regardless of the reaction of her community, a woman's status is different from the way it used to be.

Despite the diversity of ethnic groups, there are more similarities than differences among the people of southern Sudan. For instance, the Dinka and Nuer, who form the two largest ethnic groups, observe very similar cultural practices. On the eastern side of the Nile, and overflowing onto the western bank, are the northern and central Nilotic groups. The northern Nilotes comprise the Atwot, Dinka and Nuer and the Luo group of Acholi, Anyuak, Belanda, Jo-luo, Maban, Pari and Shilluk. The central Nilotes include the Bari, Jie, Latuka, Nyangatom and Toposa. In addition there are some 16 central Sudanic tribes that fall into the Bongo-Baguirmi, Kresh and Moru-Madi ethnic groups. All these groups pursue some or all of the following: cattleherding, fishing, farming. On the western side of the Nile in Western Equatoria, the Bantu-speaking Azande farmers are most numerous. They neighbour the Kakwa and Mundari agriculturists. The Didinga-speaking groups on the Uganda border are both herders and farmers.

Among the Nilotic groups, only the Shilluk and the Anyuak have a hierarchical social structure, headed by kings. The Dinka and the Nuer have a segmentary lineage system that provides leaders from among peers. All southern Sudanese view their world through the perspective of a highly specific patrilineal framework of clans, subclans and households interwoven with family and extended family connections. However, as we will see later, the war has altered these social structures in ways that directly affect women.

All southern Sudanese cultures are vigorously patriarchal and polygamous, which leads to a marked disparity between males and females. Nilotic men in particular aspire to owning many cattle, wives and children. The practice of polygamy is taken to the extreme by the Dinka of Bahr el Ghazal where it is not considered extraordinary for a man to have 30 wives. Women are responsible for the welfare of the children and the household and perform most of the chores. This leaves men free to husband cattle, fish and wage war. A woman is not an authoritarian figure within the home but is cast in the role of a kindly person who gives and receives love. Women do not own property in the sense that they control it. A woman can own a cow, but she cannot decide when or if to sell it.

Girls are regarded as a source of wealth. They are given in marriage after attaining puberty (ages vary among the different ethnic groups but the median is roughly 17 years) in return for considerable bridewealth. Among pastoral societies a groom's family, if it is rich, will pay several hundred head of cattle for a desirable bride. Among other ethnic groups, specifically those in Equatoria, bridewealth is, or was, in the form of agricultural implements, arrows and spears and other goods.[16] These days girls' families are demanding exorbitant amounts of money or the equivalent in goods. In these arranged marriages a woman remains a member of her father's lineage but she, her children and her property are controlled by her husband and, on his death, her husband's family. A woman is commonly in the position of sharing her husband with other wives. Wives who are less favoured by the husband can be penalized in the allocation of resources. This means that a wife's possessions, even if she has worked to acquire them, can be shared among the other wives at the husband's discretion. When food becomes scarce, a little-favoured woman can find that she is given far less to survive on than her co-wives. These cultural expectations have an insidious aspect for married women, as they have a lot of responsibility but little influence in directing the outcome of their actions. This is one of the great gender inequities.

One of the driving cultural premises throughout southern Sudan is that of survival through the redistribution and sharing of wealth. The linchpin for this economic and social dynamic is bridewealth. The marriage of a daughter is seen not as her individual commitment to her future husband but as a transaction that enriches the girl's family with additional resources, primarily but not exclusively cattle. These resources, in turn, strengthen bonds inside and outside the family.

It holds true for most ethnic groups that the core extended family unit is defined by the sharing of bridewealth. This unit has an obligation to protect its members in times of adversity and to share resources. Marriage also creates an alliance between unrelated families that is sealed with the payment of bridewealth by the groom's family to the bride's family. To ensure that this alliance remains firm, the payments are staggered over many years. Wealthy men reinforce their position of power by creating many alliances through marriage.

Thus women are hostage to power structures that are underpinned by material assets. A woman cannot easily leave her husband as this would signify the breaking of a carefully crafted network of assistance and obligation, within and outside the extended family, that is deemed crucial to a family's survival. Among Nilotic peoples on the rare occasions when a marriage is dissolved, the bridewealth must be returned to the man's family. Among Equatorians, bridewealth is not retrieved if there are children; in a childless marriage, it is partially retrieved. Widows are inherited by a brother of the husband so that the family assets can be kept intact. In times of peace, when customary structures are not under pressure, this practice provides a form of social security for women.

> The incidence of divorce in Toposa culture is very low. Men do not like to divorce their wives because the woman is responsible for everything, including taking care of the goats. During the dry season, women dig for water to take to the cattle. Men feel that they have paid dowry and they do not want the woman to go away. If a woman is divorced and takes her children, the husband will come and get them.
>
> Christine Lige, Narus, Eastern Equatoria

Marriage serves another function as well. A man who dies without leaving behind male children to bear his name experiences 'complete death'. The patrilineal line cannot be safeguarded unless there is sufficient bridewealth to secure another wife who will be able to conceive boys. This is achieved by conceiving girls who can be married off in return for the cattle and goods that constitute bridewealth.[17] So an important reason for a man to have wives is to conceive male children, who will perpetuate his existence through future generations.

The priority for a woman is to have children who will look after her in her old age. A woman has cultural permission to claim assistance from others on behalf of her children, rather than for herself. A childless woman is much more likely to be neglected by the community. A dramatic example of the importance of children in a woman's life occurred when Nuer attackers set fire to a Dinka hut while the children were still inside. On seeing this, the mother strode into the flames to be immolated alongside her offspring.

Large families are also deemed to have a better chance of survival than smaller families as there are more people to perform tasks. A large family is one with sufficient people to go fishing, work in the fields and look after the cattle and still have family members available to walk to the wedding of a distant relative to collect the family's due share of bridewealth while someone else treks to a far-off relief centre to collect rations.

Among the Nilotes, children are considered vulnerable until about the age of eight. After that, they are expected to do an increasing share of the household work. Boys begin to prepare for adulthood through initiation at about 11 years old. However, a girl's entry into adulthood hinges on puberty, at which point she will be prepared for marriage. Girls are not truly considered adults until they have given birth to their first child.

All these societies value their children highly and will feed them before the adults. Children belong to a number of telescoping family groups. If the parents of a nuclear family die, the children are absorbed into the larger social units to which that nuclear family belongs. Thus it is common for women to adopt orphans and take in the children of relatives. However, if villagers are forced to flee from an attack by armed men, orphans tend to be abandoned. In the midst of chaos, women look to rescuing their own children first.

Some of these traditions are still observed by some of the people some of the time. However, tradition does not hold firm when social mores and customs are no longer useful. Culture is the beliefs and customs of a social organization defined by obligations and expectations and the assignment of roles and responsibilities. A vibrant culture is one that is sufficiently flexible to be able to absorb positive adaptations and coping mechanisms to deal with crisis. But when the disaster is prolonged and excessive, the sharing and caring components of coping strategies become worn out. This in turn alters relationships between the sexes, which is what has been taking place in southern Sudan since the onset of the civil war.

At first glance, it would seem that both a woman's status and the possibilities open to her are enhanced by the level of security in the place where she lives. A gulf of opportunity separates the woman refugee in a Nairobi slum who has access to credit to start a teashop from the woman who is hiding in the swamps from marauding militia and subsisting on water lilies, a famine food. However, perceived gulf is not that simple. What ingredients constitute a woman's social and material well-being? Are women freer to make decisions about their families when surrounded by their own kinspeople even if they live in areas of conflict? Does a relatively stable environment—towns and refugee camps outside Sudan—give rise to greater opportunity for empowerment? The complex amalgam of self-esteem, security, coping mechanisms and resources must be better assessed and understood before judging what is the right mix. The balance is weighted variously in areas of conflict and relative peace inside Sudan, in camps for refugees and internally displaced persons (IDPs) and in urban areas outside Sudan.

Shifts in status, untidy and unpredictable, vary greatly according to geographic region and the intensity of conflict, but an overall picture is coming into focus. It would seem that adversity has forged a subculture of expanded self-reliance among women. It is underpinned by determination to survive at all costs and to improve frequently deplorable circumstances by exploring any avenue of opportunity that presents itself. The weakened or non-existent social safety net may have burdened women with greater hardship, but it has also rendered them ably ready for empowerment.

In places where stability exists to various degrees—Western and Eastern Equatoria, refugee camps and towns in Kenya and Uganda—women have made remarkable strides towards self-empowerment. Women across the board, including those in areas of acute crisis, have demonstrated an incredible will to better themselves. Invariably, when women living inside Sudan were asked what was needed to improve their lives, they cited education as the key to advancement, which they interpreted on a material level. They aspired to economic security through income-generating projects such as tailoring, farming, carpentry, soap-making, baking and running a small restaurant or teashop. The women said they needed money for school fees and to feed and clothe the family. Commonly, they wanted to send their daughters to school as well as their sons. The great majority of women were not consciously aware of the less tangible benefits of democratization, sexual equality and women's rights, even when it was obvious to the outsider that they were making progress in exercising those very rights.

Women's groups, which are encouraged and officially supported by the local administration, are a good focal point for

19

advancement, providing a forum for adult education classes, vocational training, credit schemes and income-generating projects. Aid agencies working with women find women's groups a useful channel for mobilizing women for workshops and projects.

Despite their considerable achievements, many women interviewed inside Sudan and in refugee camps exhibited low self-esteem. A sense of self-worth was more apparent among women who lived in urban centres outside Sudan. A prevalent self-image was a sense of inferiority to men in business and the workplace. They uniformly attributed their perceived inability to compete with men to a lack of education. It was a widely held view that education is the cure-all for women's disproportionately low representation at all levels in the administration and other decision-making organizations.

Sixty-three per cent of the population in the liberated area is female. That's why it's important to empower women so that they can help with development. Their major problem is education. It's difficult for them to know where to start and how to start. They are shy of making a mistake. Exposure to the outside world could show them what is possible and encourage them to do more. Then they can see that women are able to do things if given a chance. They are really trying. Women can do things even better than men sometimes.

David Billy, SPLM political cadre, Yambio, Western Equatoria

UN agencies, donors such as the Dutch government and NGOs are bolstering women's self-esteem through rights awareness and civil society workshops. The New Sudan Women's Federation, whose mandate is rights awareness, has trained 24 female and male paralegals to staff their offices in Yambio, Maridi, Rumbek, Bor, Mapel and Thiet. These paralegals inform women of their rights and bring cases to court where possible and appropriate. The SPLM, which has a policy of affirmative action for women, is strengthening its Family Affairs (formerly Women's Affairs) Department. The genesis of this department was at the 1994 SPLA/SPLM National Convention at Chukudum in Eastern Equatoria. Recognition that women had been marginalized was prompted by the experiences related at the convention by women who had been forced to flee their homes.[18] The first SPLM Women's Conference in August 1998 was attended by over 700 women and highlighted the need to improve the status of women and girls.

> Despite their relative larger number than men [65% of the population in the SPLA-controlled areas], the role of the female gender regrettably remained peripheral in our society in terms of effective participation in the decision-making processes in socio-political and economic issues: indeed, in all aspects of public life.
>
> Report of the Survey Team for Woman and Child Rights
> in the Context of the Legal System
> and the Judicial Structures of the New Sudan

Bonguot Amum Okic, Chief Coordinator for Gender and Development for the Sudan Relief and Rehabilitation Association, has headed the department since its inception. She is one of the privileged minority of her generation of women to have attended school. Like most of her peers, she was taught in Arabic. She learned her excellent English 'on the road'. Bonguot organizes gender workshops for both women and men, which she sees as a priority for narrowing the gap between the sexes.

> Women are coming out slowly by slowly. It's through awareness. Our men oppose the gender word. They don't know the concept. Most women haven't gone to school. Those who have, have been taught in Arabic. Offices work in English so it's difficult for them to get a job.

21

When men say women are not educated, it's false. I made a list of qualified women to show them. Now all these women are getting good positions. What's more, men must share domestic responsibilities so that women are free to go to the office. That's why we're doing women's rights.

Bonguot Amum Okic
Chief Coordinator for Gender and Development, SRRA

While some men are supportive of the promotion of women's issues, many are resistant to the idea that men and women should have greater equality. An aid worker in gender programmes points out that strong women with vision tend to be sidelined on the pretext that winning the war is the pressing objective while empowerment can be held over until the return of peace. 'Let's have liberation first and worry about women's issues later,' these men say. Suzanne Jambo, the author of a book on women's status, concurs: 'It's the educated men who oppose women's liberation, not the rural people.'[19]

The men aren't happy about these changes. They're jealous of the women's earning capacity. I tell them that the woman who is empowered is not a rebellious one. She can put the children through school and feed them so they don't go hungry. When women have a chance to do something, there is peace in the house.

Genesa Giovanna Dasta, Yambio, Western Equatoria

Negative attitudes are known to have undermined women's ability to pursue promotion within their field. There are instances of women turning down appointed or elected posts because they feel they have neither the energy nor the inclination to battle gender prejudice on a daily basis.

An example of this is the case of a well-educated woman in her 20s who stood for office in the Nairobi chapter of a male-dominated southern Sudanese organization. She was conversant with the electoral process, having witnessed it firsthand as a member of a local Sudanese women's organization. The young woman managed to garner the support of her male contemporaries, who were seeking a change of leadership, and ran such a successful campaign that she won the majority of votes. Thus, according to the constitution, she should have taken up the post of chair. Instead, the young woman chose to ask the incumbent chair, a middle-aged man, if he would remain in the post and 'teach' her. The request was deliberately made in a public forum. She was signalling that she would not threaten the organization's traditionally male authority. However, she plans to stand for chair in the next round of elections. If she wins, she intends to assume the post, having learned what the job entails from her predecessor. The majority of women are similarly of the opinion that gender reform stands a better chance of acceptance if the change is gradual rather than revolutionary.

The backlash from men is their claim that gender stuff is a foreign idea not suitable for their culture. Sudanese women who have been trained in different fields also fall back on that excuse because they find that changing attitudes to gender, when there are so few women out there, is tiring. You must appreciate that working in the Sudan is hard enough as it is. You get weary.

Aid worker, Nairobi, Kenya

legal rights

ganun aci loc piatlans – laws have rammed in the peg

Human rights apply equally to both women and men. Similarly, human rights obtain not only in times of peace but in times of

23

war. In fact, the need to respect human rights is even greater when communities are sucked into the vortex of conflict. Southern Sudan faces two problems in this context. The first is how to overlay women's rights, as defined by international conventions, on customary law when those rights contradict traditional cultural practices. The second is the application of rights when the anarchy of war has supplanted the writ of the law.

Traditional culture is held accountable through customary law, which starts at grassroots with the chief and male elders of a boma (village) court. Nilotic societies, in particular, are highly consensual. Thus customary court decisions reflect a desire to keep peace within the community rather than to safeguard individual rights. Similarly, customary court rulings uphold and perpetuate male dominance and the subservience of women to varying degrees throughout southern Sudan. At the National Convention held in Chukudum in 1994, the SPLM/SPLA introduced a set of laws entitled the New Sudan Penal Code, which holds sway in all areas under SPLA control. The penal code supersedes customary laws that are at odds with natural justice, conscience and equality. An objective of this legal system is to redress women's peripheral role in society by promulgating laws that protect some of their rights. This includes penal provision for perpetrators of crimes against women and an improvement in the custodial conditions of women convicts. In the southern Sudan of today, statutory law and customary law operate parallel to each other although statutory law overrides customary law.[20]

The enactment of laws that deal with sexual violence is a step in the right direction in affirming the rights of women. But while the SPLM/SPLA acknowledges that action must be taken to empower women, this policy statement has yet to find its way into the statute books. A SPLM directive calls for a 25% female quota in training paralegals. This quota has yet to be filled. The New

Sudan Women's Federation (NSWF), a champion of women's rights, trains male and female paralegals to work with women in their communities on sexual violence, child marriage, girls' education and related topics. Women's rights are promoted by the NSWF with the support of Oxfam and other aid agencies through rights awareness workshops. However, when asked what these rights are, both men and women regularly cite only social and economic rights such as the right to work and to education. The foundation for true development lies in the implementation of political rights. Affirmative action cannot have profound consequence until rights-based programmes promote and inculcate the concept of equal access to equal justice, equal political representation and freedom of information.

A survey conducted by an SPLM-appointed judicial committee to report on women's and children's rights found that women in Equatoria enjoyed more equality than Dinka and Nuer women. This, the team concluded, was because women in Equatoria had greater access to education. The team also noted that Equatorian men were more open to the concept of women sitting in court. The team suggested that the precedent might have been set in Equatoria by the fact that there had been examples of female chiefs in the past. By mid-2000, the only two women to sit in court in southern Sudan were to be found in a regional court and a *payam* (district) court in Equatoria. This is despite a SPLM directive that women should be represented at every Executive Chief's Court and Regional Court.[21]

Customary law regarding marriage and divorce does not favour women. For example, it is rare for a woman to get a divorce in a customary law court. If a man is impotent, arrangements are made for the woman to conceive her husband's progeny with a brother or close male relative. Neither are physical and sexual assault grounds for separation. A husband is expected to discipline his wife by beating her, and a wife is obliged to yield to her husband's sexual desires. Grounds for divorce might be found if the wife can prove that her husband is not looking after her through callous neglect or if he inflicts grievous bodily harm. A husband can sue for divorce on the grounds of repeated adultery, drunkenness and physical violence or wastage of food resources that puts the family at risk of starvation.[22]

I have two children, a boy of 13 and a girl of 15. They have been taken away from me by the father. I was divorced in court at Itang [a refugee camp in Ethiopia] in 1990 at my request. In 1991 I went to Bor but there was fighting against the Nuer. I ran to Torit and then to Kaya, moving in a big crowd. From there I went to Maridi to stay with a sister. Then Yambio, back to Kaya, then Nimule. I was always moving because there were bombs or rumours that the Arabs were coming. Then I went to Loki [Lokichoggio in Kenya] and Kakuma [refugee camp]. I discovered Abraham [the former husband] was here. He has been here since 1992 and has three other wives. He wanted to take the children so I went back to [customary] court. The court awarded him the children. Then he wanted my plot, saying it belonged to the children. The court awarded him my plot too. They said that if all divorced women could stay on their own, all women would leave their husbands. I took the ruling to the [customary] appeal court which is when my husband's brothers started coming at night to the house where I was staying to fight me. I was afraid they would kill me. I asked to be resettled in another country and I spoke to someone from the Canadian embassy. I was refused resettlement because I hadn't mentioned I have a younger half brother. I didn't know I was supposed to mention him. My children are beaten if they try to visit me. I meet my children on the way and they might be dirty, hungry, going without food. If they were with me, they would not be like that. I have tried to hang myself, but my friend stopped me.

Refugee woman, Kakuma refugee camp, Kenya

The civil administration's penal code is designed to eliminate prejudice against women and girls. So as often as not, the legal reforms are at odds with customary law. According to the code (Section 207), sexual intercourse with a girl under the age of 18 years is statutory rape regardless of whether the girl is married to the man by customary or other law. This statute is in conflict with the widespread practice of marrying girls soon after they reach puberty. Most girls are married before they reach 18. By Nuer customary law, rapists are fined a pregnant cow, a female calf and three head of cattle. When the rape is of a minor (a girl less than 14 years old), the punishment is a fine of five head of cattle and two years in jail. However, these days, rape is tried according to SPDF or SPLM laws. Among the Dinka, fines vary for raping a 'mature' girl (one heifer), an underage girl (five cows) and a married woman (six cows and a bull). All acts of rape are also liable to the penal code. The code prohibits rape (Section 208), the abetment of rape (Section 209) and assault with the intent to violate a woman's modesty (Section 196). These offences all carry jail terms with a 14-year maximum for rape although sentences of three years are more common.[23]

The penal code differentiates between 'forced' rape and 'agreed' rape. Agreed rape occurs when a girl who is a virgin has consensual intercourse before marriage. In these cases, the plaintiff is the father or the brother of the girl. Both the girl and the boy are prosecuted and both are liable to custodial sentences of up to two years. If the girl is under 18, however, the custodial sentence is suspended. Compensation to the relatives for the loss of the girl's virginity is determined by the girl's brother and the court. The court clerk at Yambio said that forced rape cases are heard about once a month while agreed rape cases are heard five times more often. This indicates that girls are still viewed as possessions. The frequency of agreed rape cases in court could show that concern for spoiling a girl's value on the bridal market is far greater than concern for a girl's physical and mental well-being.

Perpetrators of female genital mutilation, usually a female circumciser, are liable to a custodial sentence (Section 187). If a women is convicted of a crime punishable with the death penalty, the sentence is commuted if she is pregnant or suckling. Women are exempt from whipping as a punishment. A woman convicted of infanticide serves a lighter jail term than does a man who has committed the same offence.

When atrocities occur, there is no legal redress. Or at least that is the commonly held belief among civilians. While this book was being researched, several instances were cited where soldiers accused of rape had been summarily executed by military firing squad, but it was apparent that the majority of offences that soldiers committed went unreported. Rape and assault in the midst of war are inherently difficult to prosecute and the magnitude of this problem is considerable. However, if a strong regional judicial system is established and cases are prosecuted in court, it might gradually become clear to the military that they cannot rape and rob with impunity.

> As we are at war, how can we come together and make peace? It's looking quite impossible. If you have bathed your children and are in bed, even if your husband is there, men will come and knock on the door. They will ask for food. Not just ordinary food, but a chicken. If you can't help, they will force you outside and make you lie down to have their way with you. It hasn't happened to me, but I see people on the road early in the morning taking their daughters and wives to hospital. There will never be peace as long as such things happen.
>
> Name withheld, Yambio, Western Equatoria

Pursuing justice for refugees living in camps is in many ways the most challenging of all. The overburdened and underfunded judicial systems of the host countries do not reliably penetrate the perimeters of refugee camps. Customary law prevails and for the most part is welcomed by people who have been physically expelled from their homeland and yearn for the security of their own culture. At Kakuma refugee camp, women have been appointed by community leaders to the five bench (customary law) courts as part of a sexual and gender violence programme. Even so, the goal of impartial justice in cases of abduction, forced marriage and domestic assault cannot take root when customary law not only reinforces bias against the female sex but contravenes host country legislation.

The incidence of sexual violence is much more likely to decline if there is a strong judicial structure complemented by rights education. The women at Kakuma camp have furnished a solu-tion to the ill-fitting interface between customary and national law though it is uncertain that it will be implemented. They suggest that controversial judgements handed down by the bench courts be taken to the sexual and gender violence lawyer to see if they are in accordance with Kenyan law. In instances where decisions flout the law of the land, the women say, the case should be brought before the Kenyan magistrate who sits twice a month at Kakuma. Even this course of action has its pitfalls. Women do not make good witnesses in court as their culture dictates they should not speak up for themselves. And women who do take legal action against their assailants are very likely to provoke revenge assaults at the hands of those same men. The system is designed to discourage all but women of strong character. Even then, those who take up the challenge are taunted, stigmatised and threatened by the men in their community. Thus the women who are leadership material are the ones who are victimized for their efforts at reform.

workload

table 1. women's and men's roles among the Nuer and the Toposa

Tasks traditionally performed by women and girls	Tasks traditionally performed by men and boys	Tasks now performed by women and girls	Tasks now performed by men and boys
		Nuer	
. Cut grass for thatch . Cultivate . Take care of the children . Supervise children in their tasks . Ensure good home hygiene . Keep cattle pens clean . Fetch firewood . Weed . Harvest . Grind grain . Fetch water . Collect fruit during famine	. Hew wood for building houses . Smear mud on house walls . Chase away wild animals . Dig . Build the granary and fence it . Fish . Hunt . Herd the cattle . Fight in wars	. Cut grass for thatch . Cultivate . Take care of the children . Supervise children in their tasks . Ensure good home hygiene . Keep cattle pens clean . Fetch firewood . Weed . Harvest . Grind grain . Fetch water . Collect fruit during famine . Smear mud on house walls . Make fishing nets . Thatch . Dig	. Fight in the war

table continued

Tasks traditionally performed by women and girls	Tasks traditionally performed by men and boys	Tasks now performed by women and girls	Tasks now performed by men and boys
Toposa			
. Build the house . Collect produce and take it to the granary . Cultivate vegetables . Fetch drinking water . Fetch water for animals	. Go to war . Build fences . Harvest . Build the granary	. Build the house . Collect produce and take it to the granary . Cultivate vegetables . Fetch drinking water . Fetch water for animals . Harvest . Build fences . Build granaries	. Fight in the war

Source: Field research carried out by Atsango Chesoni on behalf of UNIFEM

It can safely be said that among all the ethnic groups in southern Sudan, the women have always worked much longer hours than the men. The women interviewed on this subject—Dinka, Lokonga, Lokoro, Luo (Jur), Moru, Nuer and Toposa—concurred that since the war began, this workload has increased significantly. The change in social practice, with a workday that stretches from predawn until well into the night, is rooted in a rise in the number of woman-headed households and the breakdown of traditional support systems. As clearly illustrated in table 1, women now undertake tasks that historically were allotted to men. Even so, this has not opened the door to decision-making. Rather, women have additional responsibility thrust upon them with little or none of the accompanying authority that should underpin their expanded involvement in the community. Women seldom sit on the administrative committees that oversee various communal activities. For instance, while the provision and upkeep of water supply and sanitation are deemed to be a woman's role, among the communities interviewed, only in one was there a reference to a woman's involvement in coordinating these services.

Agriculture is limited to subsistence production. Both women and men contribute in growing sorghum and cassava with the division of labour varying according to the ethnic group. The Dinka, for instance, share the backbreaking work of tilling the soil while it is customarily the women who weed and harvest. Raising livestock and fishing are men's chores. Only women collect water and firewood. Collecting wild foods is considered women's work that is beneath a man's dignity.

This division of labour directly affects women's vulnerability in times of conflict. The women's role forces them to go far beyond the safety of their homestead in search of sustenance, including relief rations from emergency feeding centres. This exposes them to physical risk from rape and assault by hostile parties. One of the reasons that the majority of landmine victims in southern Sudan are women and children is because anti-personnel mines are planted near water and firewood sources, cultivated plots and other places where people are likely to go in their business of feeding a family.[24]

There is no doubt that the war has penalized women when it comes to the division of labour. Military conscription has twisted cultural practice to free men from their traditional obligations and to chain women to a greater number of household and food security chores. It would seem that this situation has been translated into the cultural norm even where men are present to support women. Thus it has now fallen on women to perform men's tasks such as constructing huts and granaries.

The women do three-quarters of the work. We are oppressed. If you are a good woman, you wake up at 5 a.m. and prepare something that the family will eat at 7 a.m. Then you bathe the children and send them to school. This is town life. When you are in the village, you have to be careful because the place where the cattle are kept is always dirty. It is the woman's responsibility to make sure that the cattle camp is kept clean. If a child is sick it is the woman's responsibility to take it to the hospital. If you have only sons, you have to do everything. If any of the tasks is not performed, the man will fight you. Men are meant to cut wood and smear mud on the walls of the tukuls [huts]. Now they leave this work and tell us to smear the mud on the walls. Women are now even fishing. We are the ones making the fishing nets. That used to be the work of the men. Men go to the forest, thatch the roof. Their other job is to meet with ladies and produce children. The rest is done by the women.

Nuer women, Akobo, Upper Nile

Chores that have always been central to a woman's life—water collection and grinding grain—would be less onerous if there were greater access to boreholes and grinding mills. Even where boreholes exist, water collection can be extremely time consuming. Women in New Cush, living at a site where there are seven boreholes, said that the water level was so low from January to March that they had to sleep by water points to await their turn. Collection took up four to six hours of their time. As a result, during the rainy season they preferred to collect water from a nearby stream. This led to yet another chore, since the stream water contained debris and dirt that had to be filtered out.

The labour-intensive and time-consuming nature of women's work leaves them with little energy or time to engage in more productive pursuits that would improve their lives, such as income-generating projects, skills training and adult education courses. Women in Yambio, Western Equatoria, described how they rose before 6 a.m. to sweep the courtyard, fetch firewood from the forest and queue at a water point. They fed the children before school with tea or porridge then went to the market to buy greens. Women with agricultural plots of a few acres walked about 8 kilometres to till their land and returned by 5 p.m. to feed the children.

One of these women is Magdalena, a woman in her 40s or 50s who is the sole means of support for her disabled husband and their five children. She has learned how to schedule her time to improve the family's living standard. After performing the household chores, she works as an administrator at the women's resource centre until 2 p.m. Between 2 and 4:30 p.m. she attends adult education classes. She returns home to prepare and cook supper. Once the family has eaten, she prepares *godogodo* (pieces of fried cassava) until midnight. Her godogodo business allows her to earn sufficient income to pay the school fees. Because of her tight schedule, Magdalena has to subcontract their sale in the market to someone else.

education

> *My sisters are not in school because my father forbids them to go. There are 2 girls in my class and 106 boys.*
>
> Salva Majak Akoon, 11 years old

Given the extraordinary demands that are made on women in wartime, it would make sense for both sexes to have equal opportunity in education. Yet the disparity in school enrolment is enormous. The gap between girls and boys widens from 46 percentage points at the beginning of primary school to 59 points at the end. Throughout southern Sudan, women, girls and boys refer to learning as the cure-all for their problems. Yet the chance to attend school is as rare as it is sought after. It is probable that less than 15% of children of primary age are enrolled in school. Girls have always been penalized when it comes to schooling. It is estimated that 90% of women are illiterate. The likelihood of a girl pursuing her dreams by attending school continues to be dramatically less than a boy's chances. And girls in Equatoria are more likely to go to school than girls in Bahr el Ghazal or Upper Nile. Nowadays, only about 20% of the children in primary school are girls.[25]

> The most important thing is education for your child so that she is able to go far and have knowledge where she is going. If you are able to read, you can read road signs. All these years there has been no school in Mapel. Now school has just been introduced and there is no proper teaching. Education is essential for both adults and children.
>
> Elizabeth, Mapel, Bahr el Ghazal

As youngsters and women cannot depend on a male head of the family to provide the material benefits of life, they look to schooling as the key to their survival. 'Education is my mother and father' is an often-heard mantra. It is also equated with protection and safety as was revealed by unaccompanied minors at Kakuma refugee camp who were being interviewed for possible resettlement in the United States. 'In exploring the desire for education, it appears to me that children equate it as synonymous with becoming strong people who no longer need to be afraid,' said Julianne Duncan, a consultant who was conducting the interviews for UNHCR.

Southern Sudan has a long tradition of literacy and Western-type learning that dates back to the second half of the 19th century. The system was refined under British colonial rule into a 12-year, three-tier system. However, girls were virtually excluded, and the schools catered almost entirely for boys. When the war disrupted education and destroyed much of the infrastructure in the mid-

1980s, tens of thousands of boys were dispatched to Ethiopia not only to receive military training but to be educated. Very few girls were included in the group, reaffirming the widely held perception that literacy is the domain of boys while girls are destined to be the guardians of domestic routine.

The humanitarian arms of the rebel movements, FRRA, RASS and SRRA, provide educational services in much of southern Sudan with the support of UNICEF, NGOs, the churches and local communities. Yet despite creative initiatives, the challenges to providing an adequate schooling system remain. The few secondary schools are far flung and inaccessible to most youngsters. There are about 2000 community-run primary schools,[26] some of which cover only the first four years of the primary curriculum. Children often walk two to three hours a day to go to class.

About 45% of schools hold their classes in the open. Another 45% are housed in buildings constructed with local materials where pupils sit on the floor.[27] Textbooks, when available, are shared among pupils, which makes after-school study difficult. Only 7% of practising teachers have been fully trained in a teacher training college. Half the teachers have had access to an in-service course in the past decade, but only 14% had been able to complete the nine-month programme. Most do not receive any cash or other compensation for their valiant efforts, which eventually dulls their motivation. Only 7% of the teachers are women, which means that girl students do not have a positive female role model in their lives.[28]

Syllabuses are drawn from the Kenyan and Ugandan systems as well as the civil administration's 1995 syllabus. There is no accredited examining body to establish a uniform standard. This penalizes students who seek further education in neighbouring countries. Parents who have been impoverished by the depredations of war constantly struggle to pay even token school fees. And of course famine and fighting regularly force the closure of schools.

An assessment carried out by UNICEF in 2001 shows that the disparity between the sexes is far greater in areas of conflict than in areas of comparative tranquillity where educational opportunities have historically been greater. The survey offers no supporting reasons for this, but it might be assumed that education breeds a desire for more education over the generations. It is also likely that the demands made on young girls—from domestic chores to breeding more soldiers—are simply too great to allow them the luxury of literacy.

> *I am originally from Khartoum but I was displaced to Panthou by the war. My father died on the way here. I am now living with my mother. I had studied in Arabic up to P3. I am not in school now because I need money for clothes and shoes. Also the school in Panthou is in English and I was in an Arabic school. The war disrupted my education. I would like to become a doctor one day. Now I am giving Unimix at the Wet Feeding Centre. I would rather be in school.*
>
> *Elizabeth Saltata, 14 years old*
> *Panthou, a feeding camp in Bahr el Ghazal during the 1998 famine*

Difficult as it may be for youngsters to get to school, girls encounter further obstacles that are specific to their sex. This holds particularly true after the onset of puberty. In areas made inaccessible by war and geography such as parts of Upper Nile, Eastern Equatoria and Bahr el Ghazal, it is not unusual for children not to possess any clothes. Nudity in public places is embarrassing and unacceptable for pubescent girls. As schools do not provide uniforms, those without clothes have to drop out and stay at home. Girls also tend to miss school during their menstruation as sanitary pads are not available in southern Sudan. Parents are understandably reluctant to send teenage girls to schools where the only teachers are male, which is usually the case. Girls are also needed at home to take up part of the domestic burden. Youthful energy and strength are crucial assets when a mother must shoulder the workload of an absent or dead father.

Early, forced marriages are still the greatest obstacle to education for girls. Even when literacy levels among girls are comparatively high, the dropout rate after primary school is significant. In Kotobi, Equatoria, the percentage ratio of girls to boys in primary school is 38 to 62, but it falls to 5 to 95 in secondary school. Families seek a quick return on the investment they have put into raising a daughter. They want to marry her off as soon as she becomes mature. Eligibility occurs after the onset of puberty, a stage of life that usually coincides with starting to secondary school. Within this context, it would be seen as injudicious to spend school fees on a child who is shortly to belong to—and work for—another man's family.

In the eyes of the extended family, the economic value of a girl of this age, whose bridewealth represents security, far outweighs any benefits that might accrue to the girl as an individual if she were to become literate. A number of beliefs rationalizing this cultural bias have grown up around higher learning for girls: educated girls have loose morals; educated girls are disobedient; educated girls will deprive the extended family of the material rewards that are rightfully theirs. It is only in relatively stable areas, where there are more schools, that these beliefs are starting to be dispelled. For instance, in parts of Bahr el Ghazal, school leavers command bigger dowries because men recognize that an educated girl will be better at running the house.[29]

The repercussions of women missing out on education continue to result in high rates of infant, child and maternal mortality across southern Sudan. It has been repeatedly demonstrated in other countries that the better a woman's education, the more of her children survive and enjoy a better quality of life. Girls and women who have been to school have a better chance of understanding the dangers of HIV transmission and the methods of prevention as well.

Several strategies are being considered to get girls into school. The UN agencies and NGOs working in the education sector could offer reward schemes to schools that increase girls' attendance, retention and performance rates. This would mean persuading communities to change cultural values such as reducing their daughters' workloads and delaying marriage until they have finished secondary school.

Parents used to think that sending their daughters to school was a waste of time. But since 1994, the SRRA and women's groups have been trying to convince them to send their daughters to school. About a quarter of the students in school are now female. The community has recognized the value of educating their daughters. They have also realized that educated daughters are able to contribute to the family's income from their own money.

Hillary Elias, SRRA education secretary,
Mundri County, Western Equatoria

There are at least eight girls' boarding schools in southern Sudan. The oldest of these is St Bhakita in Torit, Eastern Equatoria. Since opening its doors in June 1994, it has surmounted difficult odds—drought-related food shortages, outbreaks of meningitis and cerebral malaria, aerial bombardment. About the only disruption the girls-only school has been spared is recruitment into the military.

The SRRA was running a mixed school, but it had only boys in it. I thought we needed a special effort to get the girls to go to school. Also, I believe that as long as the war is going on it is better to have schools for girls only. My experience is that mixed schools get targeted when war breaks out because the military wants boys for soldiers—sometimes they are taken by force—and this is very demoralizing.

We started under a tree and grew slowly, building with local materials. The school has no permanent donors. We depend on friends and the diocese, which buys all the textbooks and uniforms. It was only last year that we asked for feeding contributions from the parents. We have asked them to help a little. They bring firewood, and we exchange it for uniforms. Some parents are able to give a little money.

The number of students here was very high last year, when we had 500 students, but because of the drought and hunger some children went to Kakuma [refugee camp in northern Kenya] with their parents. The number is dropping now and fluctuating. It had stabilized at around 470, but with the malaria outbreak, the number is continuing to drop. I don't know how many students will be here by the time the school closes.

There are about 27 ethnic groups here. The children come from all over southern Sudan—from Yambio, Yei, Nzara. I'm constantly receiving letters requesting places for children. We decided to make the school both a boarding and a day school to accommodate the needs of the children from far away as well as encourage children from the local communities to attend. Initially we had very few Toposa girls, but now we're getting more. Another reason we had a boarding school is that the local communities are nomadic people, and when they move for grazing the children's education is disrupted. This way the children are able to continue attending school. Some of these children have also been separated from their families by the war.

The girls are happy to be in school, but when we can't get transport for them to go home, they are lonely and unhappy. We also have orphans who have no family. At least they're able to prepare for the future. They're grateful the school is there for them. We send the other children home for the holidays, except when there's insecurity. Last term we couldn't send the children of Ikotos, Chukudum and Loktok home because of the bombardments.

Sister Rita, headmistress St Bhakita, Torit, Eastern Equatoria

health

No one can function properly if they are malnourished or feeling unwell. Yet debilitation from chronic or recurring illness, overwork and improper diet is prevalent among women, particularly in areas of upheaval. There is no overt discrimination against women in the provision of medical services, but they are so burdened with the responsibility of looking after the family, typically as the single head of the household, that their ability to take advantage of what basic health care exists is curtailed. The mix of poverty, insecurity and the heavy tasks they are forced to undertake serves to undermine the health of both women and their children. Some practitioners argue that women are in less healthy condition than civilian men as a result of the war, even though there is no record of supporting evidence.[30]

Those who have been uprooted by fighting, who are on the run with little to eat, are particularly vulnerable. Women instinctively husband their energy to meet the ever-present challenge of basic survival—providing food, water and shelter for the family—with the result that basic precautions against contracting disease tend to be overlooked. Their lives are so disrupted by conflict that their ability to safeguard against illness is severely compromised.

In the absence of the traditional family network to support them in times of need, women tend to dismiss signs of illness and fatigue because, to their way of thinking, the demands of being the family caretaker outweigh the benefits of being treated. The few community clinics are far flung and likely are many miles from the homestead. Thus women seek medical assistance less frequently than men because all too often they have no one who can take care of the children in their absence.

Women who do not have a husband or male member of the family to protect their interests can face other adverse circumstances when they are away from the homestead. In a case that was told to a Save the Children worker, a Dinka war widow with four children opted against the practice of wife inheritance although she wanted to stay within the protection of her dead husband's family. Her husband's uncle's son demanded some of her cows for his bridewealth. As yet undecided on her response, she left the homestead to take her sick daughter to Panyagor for treatment. While she was away, the man took her cows and hid them. The widow took the man to court and a ruling was decided in her favour. However, the time invested in regaining her property added unwelcome pressure to her responsibilities of feeding four children and caring for a sick daughter.[31]

The health infrastructure was inadequate to meet medical requirements before the onset of hostilities. Much of what existed has since been either extensively damaged or destroyed. Some health facilities have been shelled and looted by armed militias. For instance, when Nyal was attacked in early 2001, the clinic was deliberately razed. Others have fallen into disrepair through lack of maintenance. There is a bias towards emergency relief rather than the provision of regular, long-term services. Primary health care requires an investment in water, sanitation, education, training and infrastructure.

The uneven distribution of referral hospitals reflects the difficulty of investing in areas of conflict. Western and Eastern Equatoria are the best-served regions. According to the SPLM, in 1999 there were 533 health facilities (hospitals, primary health care centres and primary health care units), which gives a ratio of just over 1:10,000. There is one doctor for every 222,000 people and roughly one nurse for every 8,000.[32]

Morbidity statistics for the global population, collated by NGOs for the year 2000, show that malaria is the disease that strikes most frequently, accounting for 27% of reported illnesses. Pneumonia, symptomatic of inadequate shelter, is the third most common disease to be treated. Diarrhoea, which ranks second among diseases treated, and typhoid, ranking fourth, are endemic. There is also a high incidence of guinea worm in Bahr el Ghazal, Upper Nile and parts of Equatoria. These illnesses can be prevented if there is access to adequate clean water. However, collecting sufficient water for washing, cooking and drinking requires multiple trips to a water source, which may be far away. As 70% of the population can obtain only unsafe water,[33] this means that additional cooking fuel must be collected if water is boiled before it is drunk. These tasks are both daunting and unrealistic for women who are already chronically exhausted.

War is frequently considered a licence for rape. This has triggered a rise in the incidence of sexually transmitted diseases. Women are reluctant and ashamed to seek medical assistance from male doctors and health workers under these circumstances. Yet medical organizations have done little to take into account female patients' modesty and cultural inhibitions by training female medical and health practitioners to examine them.[34] No data are available on the prevalence of sexually transmitted diseases, but as they are difficult to detect in women, it is likely that many sexually transmitted diseases go untreated.

There are no reliable data on the incidence of anaemia, as women do not consider fatigue sufficient reason to seek medical help. Such is their state of ill health that in most cases they do not recognize the symptoms. However, the lack of proper maternal health care indicates that anaemia must be endemic. Over 90% of women give birth at home. Two out of three deliveries take place without a medically trained person in attendance to ensure that complications are properly treated.[35] Further, recurrent bouts of malaria result in the repeated breakdown of red blood cells (an antidote to the anaemia is the consumption of cooked or fresh cattle blood, rich in iron).

The military culture that has taken root as a result of the war dictates that women are enlisted into the front to reproduce. This means that procreative practices are being driven by an imperative to replace the children who have died either in conflict or from starvation or who have been abducted by armed militias or, in the case of boys, recruited into the military. Uncertain as to when, if ever, they will next return, soldiers on home leave are determined to sire children while they can.[36] One way this change has been manifested is that enlisted husbands are transgressing a long-held taboo against sexual intercourse while a wife is breastfeeding.

Thus war has perverted the social norm for conceiving children into a no-win dilemma. The pressure to conceive at an accelerated rate invokes severe emotional anguish over choices women should not have to make. Mothers are reluctant to give birth to more children when they cannot adequately provide for the children they already have. If they attempt an abortion at home, will they die in the process? And if they die, who will look after the children they leave behind?

Certainly, the likelihood of dying in childbirth is far greater now than it would be in peaceful circumstances. Southern Sudan has one of the highest maternal mortality rates in the world: 365 per 100,000 live births. In some of the war-affected areas, this figure soars to an unacceptably high level with 865 maternal deaths for every 100,000 live births.[37]

The heavy workloads women are forced to undertake also have adverse health implications for pregnant women. The high incidence of miscarriages, as reported from Narus and New Cush, is attributed to the strenuous daily chores women must continue to perform throughout pregnancy. Two people are needed to operate borehole pumps, yet pregnant women draw water single-handedly. In places where no boreholes have been sunk, they often have to walk long distances carrying heavy loads of water. Even preparing food takes its toll. Pounding grain with a heavy pestle or grinding it with stones, bent over in a kneeling position, causes backache and chest pains, women say.

The children, too, suffer. The crucial stage of development that gives the foetus as well as the child a head start in life takes place between two weeks of conception and the first three years of life. A mother who is malnourished and anaemic and who has no access to antenatal care perpetuates the cycle of substandard health by giving birth to an underweight baby, possibly with micronutrient deficiencies. This leads to increased vulnerability to childhood diseases that would easily be preventable under normal circumstances. A sick child is yet another worrisome burden in a mother's fight for survival. In southern Sudan the death rate among children is unusually high: 110 cases of infant mortality and a further 145 cases of death among under-fives for every 1000 live births.[38] In reality, this figure is much higher as many deaths go unreported.

Against this background, it is surprising that women seldom cite ill health or inadequate medical services when asked to itemize their problems. The fact that they appear to be resigned to operating at a subnormal level of well-being underlines how commonplace the phenomenon is. Women and their young children are certainly hardest hit by the war-induced disruption of health services.

recommendations

- UN agencies and NGOs should foster women's and men's awareness of women's human rights not only through workshops for both sexes but also by incorporating civic education components into projects and by ensuring that women participate in planning and monitoring their projects.
- Civil society should be encouraged to introduce and strengthen penal codes that are impartial in meting out justice

and that eliminate prejudice against women and girls, particularly with respect to sexual violence and property ownership. When customary law is applied, those laws should enshrine the rights of women.

- Girls should have equal access to equal education, which includes the introduction of many more female teachers and headmistresses into the educational system. This would hasten the eventual elimination of the negative aspects of customs such as the manipulation of women and girls through the mechanisms of bridewealth and widow inheritance.

- UN agencies, NGOs and civil administrations should support healthier women and their children and babies by ensuring access to clean water, health clinics and mother-and-child health care, by monitoring the prevalence of sexually transmitted diseases. To accomplish these aims, more female medical and health practitioners must be trained.

women's status in and out of war zones

women in areas of stability

Western Equatoria and Lakes are considered stable in contrast to other parts of southern Sudan, which are either conflict prone or potentially insecure. It is in these areas of comparative tranquillity that aid agencies have implemented limited development pro-grammes through supporting the construction of schools and clinics and by introducing agricultural and income-generating projects.

Yambio in Western Equatoria is one of the towns considered stable enough to be the focus of development interventions. The SPLM seized control of the town from the government in 1990 and began rehabilitation the following year. Since then the town has been bombed only twice, a remarkable record given the widespread aerial bombing campaigns. This relative stability has allowed women to organize and make greater advances in their lifestyle than their contemporaries in other parts of southern Sudan. With an initial impetus from churches, women were soon organizing women's groups in all the payams of the county. Then, with the encouragement of SPLM officials, they began to pursue opportunities for adult education and income generation. Women said that with their husbands away at the front, they needed to become the family breadwinners. And to do that, they said, they had to go to school as at least 75% were illiterate. The women of Yambio built a resource centre consisting of several mud-and-thatch rooms. They wanted the resource centre to be self-sufficient so a wing was added that caters for outside visitors who come to Yambio for workshops and meetings. They use the resource centre as a meeting place where they can discuss credit schemes and other issues of cooperation. The resource centre also provides a classroom for adult literacy and business skills.

In 1993 an international NGO established an office in Yambio and distributed seeds. As the area is fertile, the seed enabled the women to cultivate onion, cabbage and other vegetables, which they sold in the marketplace. The same NGO brought in sewing machines and distributed one apiece to women's groups in six payams. Then the women bought material with money earned from the sale of their vegetables. Since the disappearance of merchants from the north at the beginning of the war, people were dressed in rags. The NGO taught them tailoring skills as there was a great demand for clothes. Soon the acquisition of other skills followed: carpentry, soap-making, tie-and-dye, baking and catering. All these income-generating projects were assisted by international NGOs.

This war has changed things for us. Before we were confined to the house. We would not be sitting at a sewing machine or baking bread or running a restaurant in the marketplace. In the old Sudan, only men did tailoring. No one would believe that women could do that thing.

Genesa Giovanna Desta, Yambio, Western Equatoria

The women suffered setbacks. Delighted with their achievements, they decided to expand their businesses by buying supplies in neighbouring Uganda, a day's drive away during the dry season if all went well. This would have severed dependency on the NGOs that had been supplying the materials. At this point the women came up against their business competitors, all of them men. The male traders offered to give the women lifts on their trucks on the understanding that they would pay for the ride and for all the 'taxes' that would be demanded at roadblocks along the way. Given the low turnover of the women's businesses, they decided that buying wholesale in Uganda was not feasible. The women did not talk of creating a buying cartel, which would have given them more leverage when negotiating prices with the men.

Then in March 2000, the NGOs that had been supplying the raw materials withdrew from Yambio as they had opted against signing a Sudan Relief and Rehabilitation Association memo of understanding on their operating terms in southern Sudan. Now women rely on the male traders, who supply them their raw materials at inflated prices. Thus their male rivals have effectively obstructed the women's plans for business expansion. The women say they want to purchase their own truck but fear that it would be appropriated by soldiers during one of its trips to and from Uganda. In reality, as there are no banks and few other sources of credit, the women would be unlikely to find the financing for this venture. Some women have started their own revolving credit schemes. The amounts involved are very small and the return on investment is less than a week.

We are a group of five who want to plan for something. We start with a contribution of SDP 500.* We have small papers with 'yes' and 'no'. There is only one 'yes'. We make a vote. We just roll up the paper and put it on the ground. If you get a yes, the money is going to be handed to you. You will start business with this SDP 2,500. You must return the money after seven days. You bring the amount back with the profit. That profit goes to you. Then we do a vote again. All of us are doing it to improve our living standard, and all of us have capital to work with. We started last year. Most of us do godogodo [fried cassava pieces] because it's cheaper and more fast. Then we go to making bread. I use the profit to buy a packet of flour to make bread. Then we sell tea with

---

* Sudanese pound, valued at 550 to USD 1 in 2002. The Sudanese pound is not legal tender in Government of Sudan areas.

the bread so the money is growing. This year I started a farm with the money. I grow maize, soya beans, simsim.

Magdalena, Yambio, Western Equatoria

Women who are out of the areas of fighting have exhibited keen entrepreneurial instincts. Their understanding of business practices is limited, however, as demonstrated by their failure to break the Uganda trading cartel that remains in the hands of the men. The emergence of credit schemes shows that these women are motivated by visible rewards. Even so, women also have the vision to pursue other objectives. In Yambio, 14 local women contributed money to start a local branch of the New Sudan Women's Federation. This office employs paralegals to safeguard the rights of women in the community. However, this is a far less tangible benefit than access to credit.

women in crisis-prone areas

The prospects for self-improvement in areas where fighting is going on are narrow compared with opportunities in areas that are more or less free of fighting. Debate continues among aid agencies as to whether empowerment through development activities and gender workshops should be introduced alongside relief operations. There are those who argue that it is futile to introduce income-generating skills and rights awareness among women who are constantly being forced to flee the military. The daily struggle to subsist is too great to allow them to focus on activities that reach beyond basic survival. Others are of the opinion that women should have the opportunity to become mistresses of their own destiny. Those who subscribe to the 'development amid relief' school of thought suggest that women who are members of a community, no matter how fragmented that community may be, are the ones who will provide the crucial keystone for peace building.

Interviews conducted at Nyal in Upper Nile with members of the Women's Association for Leech State highlighted the uncertain existence of women who live in areas of sporadic hostilities. Half the women in the group, all of whom were Nuer, were war widows.

> *We came from Kaoch where there was fighting three years ago. When the Dinka come, you just run. You don't know where you are going. You hide in the swamps for a night or two days but to cross the swamp is very difficult because you don't have a boat. For a woman, it is very difficult to carry all your children. You must leave everything else behind. There is no [drinking] water, no food. You just have to trust in God. When we came here, we were happy to see there is no fighting. At Kaoch there are no tukuls because people are always moving around.*
>
> Elizabeth Chol, Nyal, Upper Nile

The interviews were held in the open next to the Relief Association of Southern Sudan office. It is customary for RASS officials, all men, to attend such gatherings, but they were asked if they would stay away. The request was honoured, probably because the interviewer was perceived to be 'a foreign aid worker'. It is worth noting that this meeting was the first time that any of the women had ever been asked to give their views in an entirely female forum, which allowed them to be far more open. The occasion was deemed so extraordinary that each woman individually commented on it and thanked the interviewer for giving her the opportunity to express herself freely.

Despite their precarious situation, these women demonstrated clarity of purpose and vibrant, logical thinking when articulating their aspirations. Unsurprisingly, all were tired of war and voiced a desire to be part of the decision-making process so that they could promulgate unity that would lead to peace.

We have two requests. I would like to ask if there are other women's groups with similar problems. If so, we want to know if it is possible to all get together to discuss our problems. We also want [the means] to earn some money. We would like dyes and materials to make tie-and-dye clothes to sell in the market. The men want to buy tie-and-dye clothes. We can distribute the materials to women's groups in the region by dugout canoes. We also need seeds—Irish potatoes, tomatoes, okra and murendaa [a small-leafed chard]—to grow vegetables for sale.

Mary Nyandio, chairwoman,
Women's Association for Leech State, Nyal, Upper Nile

A case can be argued for allocating such materials amid the ebb and flow of conflict. Nyal, which was under the jurisdiction of the SPDF, had not been bombed or attacked for at least five years and was considered an island of tranquillity. Within days of the interviews taking place, the village was overrun by the SPLA and razed. Hopefully, the women interviewed managed to hide safely in the swamps just as they did when they fled Kaoch three years earlier. In due course, they will have emerged to make a cautious return to Nyal or to move on to another place that they believe to be more secure. Wherever they settle, be it for a few months or several years, it can be presumed they will not have lost sight of their ambition to sell vegetables and tie-and-dye clothes. In fact, given that they must have had to abandon all their material possessions, the chance to restart their lives by earning money will have become even more vital to their survival. All women interviewed for this book, no matter what their circumstances, confirmed that having an income is a primary objective. Life becomes considerably easier when there is access to modest start-up materials to begin a small business, they said.

Women's commitment to economic independence, even when they must regularly flee conflict, is continually being demonstrated.

For instance, the women of Mabil in Bahr el Ghazal's Aweil County still manage to earn small amounts of money even though the chronic insecurity makes it impossible to organize women's associations. The women weave and sell mats, which they also use for their own shelter. They collect firewood for sale. They make mosquito nets from sacks and string from grass to use for thatching. They make brooms and pots and decorate gourds. All of these activities use only local raw materials and so are sustainable despite the women's high mobility. There is a ready market for their wares as they are selling basic household utensils and construction materials for people's homes. It can be argued that insecurity creates the market, as each time populations flee and a village is razed, people must start building their homes from scratch.

The case history of the Nyal women underscores the difficulty of planning even short-term development assistance, given the unpredictable dynamics of hostilities. On the other hand, the benefits of rights awareness along with income-generation and conflict-resolution skills are permanent and cannot be lost, even on the run. To break free from the restrictions placed on their sex, women need exposure to role models who have already achieved this and the encouragement and know how to follow their example. This knowledge is internalized to become an indivisible part of what motivates a woman. Education not only provides the building blocks for a better future, it restores hope by allowing a woman to reclaim her dignity. Thus there is a pragmatic rationale for organizing gender and development workshops in areas of crisis.

We are tired of this relief syndrome. Most women have been in war a long time and need development. Development can't be done without human resources. They need training in skills, and they need to learn English so they çan enter the education system.

Sitouna Abdalla, Chairwoman,
New Sudan Women's Federation, Nairobi, Kenya

internally displaced women

Sudanese throughout the south have adopted mobility as a coping mechanism. However, it is a strategy of last resort. Abandoning home, cattle, fields and fishing grounds is an admission that all other coping mechanisms have failed. The current estimate of about 4 million gives Sudan the largest number of internally displaced people in the world. The great majority are women and children.

Displacement patterns shift like a kaleidoscope. They are triggered by warfare between southern rebel factions and government military, interfactional fighting between ethnic groups, raids by armed militias from the north, flooding and famine. Assessments are further complicated by nomadic migration patterns and large-scale movements of the population in search of emergency assistance. For instance, the situation worsened in 1998 when the effects of a major famine were compounded by heavy fighting in and around Wau in Bahr el Ghazal.

More recently, human rights violations have forcibly expelled people from their homes in areas where foreign oil companies have exploration and extraction rights. The hardest hit locations are in Western Upper Nile, the site of three oil concessions operated by consortiums of the Sudanese government and foreign partners. The China National Petroleum Corporation leads the consortiums, drilling at Heglig and Unity oil fields in partnership with the Malaysian state-owned Petronas Bhd, Canada's Talisman Energy and the Sudanese government's Sudapet. Lundin Oil AB of Sweden is the lead partner for the oil field at Thar Jath. By February 2001, the number of displaced in this area had increased from 29,230 to more than 36,500 in the space of a year.[39]

There was bombing all the time and those who survived were shot by government soldiers coming on foot. Even my husband was killed. I have been going on foot for three months, carrying my daughter Monica. She's two.

Elizabeth Henry, 19, from Gogrial, Bahr el Ghazal

Famine poses a threat for people who have been dislocated by conflict, as the enemy commonly burns crops and loots livestock. When the government bans OLS flights to these areas, as happened in Western Upper Nile on several occasions from 1999 through 2001, the prospect of widespread starvation becomes even more grave. Isolation from marketplaces and health services because of deteriorating security temporarily displaces women and children, rather than men, as they migrate to relief centres. Another cause of migration to relief centres is when food becomes scarce and polygamous husbands allocate available food in a way that discriminates against some of the wives. In this instance, it is usually the junior wives who trek to relief centres to find food.

Displacement, in many ways at the cutting edge of social change, puts extreme pressure on social systems. To survive, people who have been locked into a tightly knit structure of subclan relationships must suddenly learn to deal with people to whom they are not related. They find this difficult. Women's battle for empowerment is probably hardest among the displaced. Discrimination is heightened among women who have no male head of family to defend their status. And sexual violence can be rife when perpetrators know there is no one to whom women can report the violations.

Two IDP camps were visited during the study: Narus and New Cush in Eastern Equatoria. Groups of internally displaced women in Akuem, Mabil, Mapel and Panthou in Bahr el Ghazal were also interviewed. The women had certain things in common. They identified their basic needs as shelter, water, household utensils and food. When running away from danger, the women left behind mosquito nets, cooking utensils, blankets, clothing and seed for planting. Other concerns were the lack of social amenities, the insecurity and the breakdown of support systems for the most vulnerable women. Many women introduced skills into the camps. In Mabil, two of the women were the only female teachers in Aweil County. In Mading and Narus, women had started women's organizations and were training other women in new skills.

Many women have been on the move for nearly 20 years. Despite this, they have acquired skills and manage to put them to use. This supports the argument that even when women are mobile, they fare better when given development opportunities. Women's testimony indicated that the quest for education is an important motivator for their wanderings as well as the search for security and food.

> *I am originally from Yei. Between 1983 and 1990 I lived in Kobe. When Kobe was shelled, I moved to Lokreji. It was a newly liberated area, and the people in the movement kept disturbing us for girls to be their wives. Life became very hard. We moved to another place near DRC [Democratic Republic of Congo]. Life there was difficult. We had food, but there were no education facilities. So we decided to move to Kaya. There were education facilities, but as soon as the children would turn 11, the boys would be taken to join the movement and the girls would be married off. At night we would pretend we were washing clothes and smuggle our children to Koboko in Uganda. I got involved in a small business selling clothes. I fell sick with typhoid. It coincided with the death of my brother. My sister, who lives in Nairobi, attended my brother's funeral and learned that I was sick. She collected my daughter, niece and me. An aid organization in Kenya gave the children scholarships. I was trained in tailoring and tie-and-dye. In 1997 I got a job with an aid organization and went to Yei to work on agroforestry. Now I am working with another aid organization, teaching tailoring to the Narus Women's Group.*
>
> *Eunice, Narus, Eastern Equatoria*

A study of the interaction between displaced and resident communities conducted in northern Bahr el Ghazal at Akon and its satellite villages between November 1993 and February. 1995 analyses the pitfalls of displacement.[40] During the 1989 famine, an IDP camp was established at Akon for Dinka from Aweil and Gogrial districts. The camp population of some 20,000 fluctuated as and when people migrated to other relief centres or considered it safe to return home. On average, the IDP population was 10 times greater than the host population in Akon.

The displaced lived in makeshift huts erected in the spaces between residents' houses. The great majority of IDPs belonged to a different Dinka subsection than did the Akon residents. Even kinship ties among the displaced were tenuous to non-existent. While IDPs established cooperating mechanisms among themselves, there were tensions with the host community, who resented having to share their resources with strangers.

The study cast light on the role of kinship and its effect on women in coping with their circumstances, their vulnerability, and their access to and control of resources in war zones. Women excelled in survival over men in a variety of ways. They made considerable effort to reinvent their status to compensate for vanishing guidelines governing female–male relations. They took up the slack when there was no male to contribute to household food security. They sought support outside the failed kinship network. Many female-headed households relied heavily on wild-food gathering and conducted small businesses such as selling beer, timber, firewood and grass to expand their resources.

The survey showed that the displaced were more impoverished and less able to draw on kinship support than Akon residents. The exchange of cattle is pivotal to reinforcing social, economic and political standing in Dinka society. Therefore it was axiomatic that the displaced, who had lost most of their livestock, had little leverage in exacting mutual dependence between kin as their means of reciprocity was non-existent.

Among the displaced women surveyed, only a third were accompanied by the male head of household. The others were war widows, junior wives whose husbands had discriminated against them in the allocation of household food, and women whose husbands were either fighting or had migrated north in search of a means of making money. This group led an even more precarious existence than those with husbands present because they were unable to elicit economic support from kinship affiliations; 20% of the female-headed households were considered vulnerable.

Some women complained that their families were malnourished or starving even though their lineage kin were well off. This may have been because war-induced resource deprivation has placed such stress on the tradition of kinship caring and sharing that the kinship affiliation is now viewed from a more selfish perspective. The study suggests that contemporary Dinka men regard kinship as a means of pinpointing their place in the social hierarchy rather than as a basis for social interaction. Whatever the reason, non-kin relationships were more 'enduring and trustworthy', the women said. These non-traditional social ties were created with representatives of the displaced, through child-care networks and income-generating groups.

The disintegration of the extended and nuclear family structure had a negative impact on children too. Infant malnourishment was not necessarily directly related to milk and grain shortages. Mothers who were forced to spend long hours gathering food in the wild had less time for breastfeeding. This in turn led to premature weaning and malnutrition.

I could not harvest enough grain last agricultural cycle because of drought and because a woman's hands alone cannot produce sufficient food for a family of six. I do not own any livestock because we were raided four years ago and that makes my life more difficult compared to other households back in my village. The relatives of my husband have cows but are unwilling to support us. You know that ngong [poverty] changes people's morality. [There is] no one to give me a hand in the fields. The man of my house [husband] went to the north just before the start of the last cultivation season. He was embarrassed by the fact that he could not provide for his family and so he decided to leave.

Displaced woman, Akon, northern Bahr el Ghazal

It was found that when relief organizations targeted poor households, they further penalized displaced people, particularly women, as they tended to constitute the majority of what was considered to be the vulnerable population. The 'privilege' of external assistance fanned simmering resentment among the host community. When agencies ceased emergency deliveries, those who were most in need of support—the recipients of the relief supplies—were the least likely to get it. The Akon residents' animosity towards the displaced precluded them from any assistance that otherwise might have come from within the community.

These people brought here by [the] UN, and the building of the airstrip, have deformed the face of our village. They defecate all over and they compete with our people over drinking water so it is better they return to their homes and come back here only on the days of distribution.

Local administrator responsible for relief distribution, Akon, Bahr el Ghazal

Even though emergency programmes for IDPs may have caused social rifts and tremors, there was no doubt that they benefited the women and children who were targeted. Feeding centres provided wet feeding (essentially porridge) for the children and grain for the mothers. Without this assistance, many would have died.

women in refugee camps

Over the years, hundreds of thousands of southern Sudanese women have sought safety in refugee camps run by UNHCR. At the beginning of 2001, more than 490,000 Sudanese, the majority of them women and children, were registered with UNHCR. Some fluctuate between Sudan and the camps in neighbouring Central African Republic, Chad, the Democratic Republic of Congo, Eritrea, Ethiopia, Kenya and Uganda, swept back and forth by the ebb and flow of conflict. Others settle into a particular camp and remain there for years.[41] For these exiles who have opted against returning home until there is peace, the future can look bleak, which inevitably colours their outlook on life. No in-depth assessments have been made of the mental health of refugees. However, when refugee women speak, it becomes clear that a great number are chronically depressed and even suicidal. Women also contend with suppressed anger, which neither the system nor their culture allows them to vent. This state of mind has a corrosive effect on their coping mechanisms.

> We flee the Sudan and our problems follow us. The security is fine but it's an alien environment—hot and windy, no grass or rain or water. We get homesick for familiar surroundings. Most people who came here have died even though there's a hospital. The place where they bury people is full. Now they have started another one.
>
> Martha Nyadier, a Bor Dinka, Kakuma refugee camp, Kenya

Women refugees' sense of disempowerment is not imaginary. The inhabitants of refugee camps may have the basic necessities of life—food, shelter, primary education and health care—but they are deprived of the freedom of choice. No lifestyle decision can be made without recourse to a higher authority. UN and NGO staff oversee the administration of food distribution, education, health, water, sanitation and other community services. Decisions and regulations can be at variance with the refugees' culture back home. Sudanese committees, organized along ethnic lines, deal with grassroots community affairs, including disputes and cases of potential or committed violence. These elected community committees remain an exclusively male domain that exercises a patriarchal bias when adjudicating controversy. Thus refugee women are hostage to the discriminatory practices of their society.

> If we ask in the day to be represented on the committees, in the evening, the men will beat us. The men say, 'Is it because of the war that women think they can talk to the men?' If a man beats his wife, she used to take it to [the] gender [officer working for an NGO]. [The] gender [officer] takes it back to the community. So the person who is supposed to solve that problem is the person who used to beat his wife too.
>
> Refugee woman, Kakuma refugee camp, Kenya

Women arrive in refugee camps already greatly traumatized by hardship and loss. They may have walked for months through hostile territory, subsisting on wild fruits and herbs and drinking water from puddles. Often the weaker members of their family, particularly their children, had died along the way. Having fled the chaos of war that engulfed their homes, all too often they find that their problems have followed them across borders to their place of supposed refuge. Against this background, it is easy to see how a woman living in a refugee camp can succumb to despair.

Living as they do at one remove from their clan structure, refugee men can transgress accepted moral and ethical behaviour with impunity. Based on case histories gathered from refugee women, there is strong evidence to suggest that refugee men pervert established cultural codes of conduct to perpetuate and safeguard their own interests. Many women live in daily terror of domestic beatings that are exacerbated by cramped living conditions. Girls who are in the care of refugee foster families are prevented from attending school and forced to stay at home to perform all the household chores. Too often they are subjected to physical and sexual assault. Orphaned or separated from their families, these youngsters do not know where to turn for help. Women who complain to the community elders are publicly mocked and their pleas for protection ignored. Some girls and women become so distressed that they contemplate hanging themselves as the only way out.[42]

According to women at Kakuma refugee camp in northern Kenya, a woman who has been subjected to physical assault can report the incident to the community 'police' (Sudanese refugee men who act as grassroots security officers). If the assailant is not the woman's husband, he is required to appear before the community bench (customary law) court. The court may fine the accused USD 0.65 a day for up to seven days according to the severity of the beating. But if the assailant is the woman's husband, there is no case to be heard. These courts, moreover, are illegal as refugees, like all residents of Kenya, are subject to the laws of the land.

Kakuma refugee camp lies 120 kilometres from the Sudanese border. With over 60,000 refugees living in mud-brick houses sprawled across the barren landscape, it is like a small city, with all the accompanying social pressures. Most of the population is from Ethiopia, Somalia and Sudan. Sudanese are the most numerous with Dinka constituting by far the largest ethnic group. Women greatly outnumber men and most are single heads of household. Deprived of the protection of the extended family, they are unusually vulnerable.

These women are subjected to what is possibly a unique form of sexual violence: abduction of women and their children by male family members who have come to take them back to the Sudan to be married. Women are looked upon as a lucrative resource to be traded in marriage for cattle, a highly valued commodity. Given the high attrition rate of herds because of war and natural disaster, it is easy to see why men are eager to rebuild their herds and recover their status by marrying off all female members of the extended family. Women who have fled to refugee camps are no exception.

The case of Sara, a beautiful and courageous young Dinka who lives at Kakuma, is typical. A much-loved wife and doting mother, she is nevertheless anxious and fearful. At night she sleeps little, anticipating the soft slap of sandalled feet approaching through the darkness. The source of Sara's anguish is her own brother, a man she has not seen since she was a little girl. He has walked from the family homestead in Sudan to encamp near her mud house. His mission is to take Sara back to Sudan and force her into marriage with a man she has never met. Sara's brother claims her husband has defaulted on the bridewealth of cattle he agreed to pay. Therefore Sara's husband no longer has the right to 'own' her. Shortly after the couple's marriage, they trekked to Kakuma. The possession of livestock is prohibited in the camp so her husband cannot pay his bridewealth instalments. Now, eight years later, Sara is being reclaimed for marriage to someone wealthier who can provide the 50-odd head of cattle required for Sara's dowry. Sara's resistance has made her brother angry. He has threatened to kill her husband. He says he will seize the children. He knows if he abducts her young son and daughter and the suckling baby he can force Sara to follow.

Sara has placed her trust in an NGO social worker, but there is little the social worker can do except bring her case to the attention of UNHCR's protection officer. She, too, is constrained in her actions, faced with the dilemma of preventing a crime that has yet to take place. Sara is a leading member of her local women's support group, one of 40 that have been established by the women. These are all useful forums for discussing the prevention of violence and persecution, but these groups exercise no authority and little influence. Abductions and other forms of violence are illegal under Kenyan law, and perpetrators should be prosecuted. However, there will be no significant change in the status of women refugees until they are encouraged to stand for election to the administration committee that governs the day-to-day affairs of refugee communities and when those responsible for the refugees' security take threats of violence against women seriously.

Sara is not alone in her helplessness. Statistics on the various forms of violence directed against Sudanese women do not exist, but it is accepted that abductions are commonplace. The difficulties of verifying cases where threats are involved are well known, but protection should extend beyond committed abuses to include the high-risk possibility of abuse. This means preventive action must be taken before physical assault takes place.

UNHCR has acknowledged women's specific needs and begun to translate that into action. UNHCR staff at Kakuma have been particulary active in introducing gender and rights awareness and seeking ways to curb sexual abuse. For instance, a safe haven has been built. At the time of publication, it had yet to become operational, but when it does open its doors, women under threat of violence will be able to seek temporary refuge there.

A sexual and gender violence lawyer runs a sexual violence programme. Her legal advice clinics average an attendance of 40 to 60. Sessions are conducted in the afternoons, when there is a lull in community activity, and can be as frequent as nine times a month. Participants are asked to nominate the topic of discussion. Community leaders, all of whom are male, are encouraged to participate so that they can be equipped with the legal knowledge that will help them to deal fairly with cases of sexual violence committed against women.

Another reform is the introduction of a mobile court, representing the Kenyan judicial system, that sits at Kakuma twice a month. While other nationalities take advantage of this court, it is rare for Sudanese women to pursue cases through the system. Victims of sexual violence are reluctant to prosecute assailants, fearing that the suspect will seek revenge once he has served his jail term. However, in November 2000, the first abduction case was heard in court. The complainant, Elizabeth Nyanjo Chionco, said that her relatives, Geu Jok and Abraham Thiu, had kidnapped her twin boys with the intent of taking them to their father, who was in Sudan. This was the second abduction attempt made on the children. Geu Jok pleaded guilty and was sentenced to three years and six months in jail. Abraham Thiu, who pleaded not guilty, was found to be an accomplice and given a six-month custodial sentence. Unlike other cases, Elizabeth got her sons back. It is hoped that this precedent and the cases that follow will be a deterrent to men who want to force their sisters and daughters into unwanted marriage.

The protection of women is improving, but more slowly than the proponents of gender equality would like. The fault line remains between entrenched attitudes and recently promulgated UN conventions to safeguard women's rights. Refugee women still have virtually no say in the affairs of their community. And, for the most part, men like it that way.

In Sudan, we keep silent until we die. Now we are here, we want to change our culture.

Nyiel, Kakuma refugee camp, Kenya

urban refugees

Most refugees cross from Sudan to Kenya, Uganda and Ethiopia on foot and make their way to camps situated near the border. But a small percentage manage to live in urban areas in Uganda and Kenya. There are Sudanese refugees living in Arua, Eldoret, Jinja, Kampala, Kapenguria, Kisumu, Kitale, Nairobi, Nakuru and other towns. Those who arrive in urban centres tend to have had some schooling and to be economically better off as is reflected in their ability to travel long distances by air or road and to stay in town, which is expensive compared with a refugee camp.

UNHCR's mandate is to promote the integration of refugees with the host country.[43] However, countries that have a large burden of refugees find it difficult to accommodate influxes of indigent foreigners into society. In Uganda, legislation allowing refugees to live where they choose is in the process of being enacted. Meanwhile, the government allows refugees who can afford to live in towns to do so. In Kenya the authorities require refugees to live in one of two designated and isolated refugee camps—Dadaab and Kakuma. Refugees who reside in Nairobi and other towns require the approval of UNHCR to do so. The common reasons for residing in an urban area are for medical treatment, higher education or because a woman's security has been consistently threatened in the camp. No official data are available, but probably hundreds of women live in Nairobi and other towns without any legal documentation.[44]

Usually, urban refugees have access to resources such as education, transport and housing. They are able to move about freely, live with their families and send their children to school. In short, their life is relatively normal, a blessing that is not conferred on the majority of southern Sudanese women. In Kenya, it is common for urban refugee women of other nationalities to suffer at the hands of authorities, who take advantage of the fact that they have little recourse to the legal processes because of their 'vulnerable' situation. However, southern Sudanese women are rarely subjected to harassment because of the comfortable relationship the SPLA enjoys with the Kenya government.

This is not the case elsewhere. In Eritrea, when relations with the Khartoum government warmed up, southern Sudanese refugees who had been living peacefully in Asmara were summarily moved to Haikota, a trucking stop in the western desert, where they were confined to an enclosed camp a few kilometres outside the town. The women complained they had so little to eat that they had no milk to breastfeed their babies.[45] This discriminatory behaviour is in violation of the 1951 Convention Relating to the Status of Refugees and the 1969 OAU Convention on the Specific Aspects of Refugee Problems in Africa.

Despite this, women living in towns as refugees have far greater access to the resources offered by NGOs and aid agencies than their counterparts inside Sudan. They can seek opportunities to improve themselves in ways that are not available to women in camps. As a result, their self-esteem grows as they learn new skills that bring them a better standard of living. They can mix freely with society at large and are, to a large extent, able to influence the course of their daily life. This instils the confidence that presages evolving attitudes and leadership.

The considerable achievements of these urban women have provoked reactions among their men. At first they were sceptical, but now they are supportive of the women's initiatives. These women will be important role models for other women when they return to Sudan. Even before a peaceful resolution to the conflict has happened, they could be tapped as a development resource. It has been suggested that urban refugee women train trainers who are living in southern Sudan. This would allow the benefits of the skills they have acquired to trickle down to grassroots level in a cost-effective way.[46]

Women's associations such as the Sudanese Women's Association in Nairobi (SWAN) are multifaceted. They provide a base for networking among urban women and are the source of initiatives to seek solutions to common social and economic problems. Nurses talk to mothers about the benefits of vaccinations. Nutritionists advise on how to provide a nutritious diet from low-cost food.

Just as important, exile becomes a training ground for a better post-conflict life in Sudan. Since SWAN was registered in 1994, its members have had access to credit for small businesses, training in tailoring, literacy and English courses, and personal and institutional capacity building. They have also learned about advocacy, the electoral process and civic procedures. All activities stress the peace-building techniques of cooperation, collaboration and consensus.

Putting policy into practice, SWAN has 21 neighbourhood communities, each with its own chairwoman. These are overarched by an executive committee consisting of six women who have been elected by a general assembly that constitutes all the members.

Working groups are restricted to 29 women to ensure that interaction takes place among all the members. The women speak in their own languages during discussions and group members translate for each other. Each group elects a chair, treasurer and secretary. When there is disagreement, they reach a solution by consensus. Underlying all this is the message that the organization is a community where women are there to support each other.

We came together so we would not fight in a strange land as our husbands are fighting. It doesn't matter who our husbands are. We share the same problems. In working together the strangest love affairs develop. We don't speak evil of our men. When someone tries to do that, the woman is surrounded and escorted to the gate.

Pauline Riak, executive director of SWAN, Nairobi, Kenya

According to Pauline Riak, SWAN emphasizes a woman's economic independence on the premise that survival precedes democracy. Thanks to the organization's revolving fund, members have become taxi drivers, butchers, dealers in secondhand clothes and the owners of vegetable kiosks. Others make tie-and-dye cloth or peanut butter or school uniforms for both Kenya and Sudan. The fund has a 90% repayment record. Members who are mired in debt are accorded forgiveness on their loan obligations. Initially, loans were for KES 3,000 but this was insufficient to rise above subsistence. Now loans are for KES 30,000 and sometimes more.*

My husband is a SPLA commander. I finished junior secondary school and then stopped to get married when I was 18.˙ He left me in the bush in 1987 when he went to fight. In 1990 I took a UN plane from Juba and came to Nairobi with my children. I have four. Three are in primary school and one is in nursery. My husband sends me money every month. UNHCR sponsored me at a tailoring school. They gave me an allowance of KES 900 a month. I studied for four years. I was selling peanut butter for money. Friends helped me too, and I walked around to offices asking for help. In 1995 I opened a business in Kenyatta Market selling materials and tailoring. I applied for a loan from SWAN because I wanted to expand to a larger shop. I wanted to buy materials in Uganda and another sewing machine and hire another helper. I sell kitenges [African cloth] and tie-and-dye dresses and men's African clothes. My customers are Kenyans and Zairois [from the Democratic Republic of Congo]. I even export to Sudanese who have resettled in the United States. When I asked for a loan, I was interviewed first. Then I had to do training for three and a half days. In February I got a loan of KES 30,000. Then in September I got another loan of KES 25,000. The

---

˙ Kenya shilling, valued at KES 78 = USD 1 in 2002.

interest rate is 10%. It's easy to pay back. The extra money I make goes to the kids.

Betty Poni Simon, Nairobi, Kenya

Other indigenous Sudanese NGOs have a presence in Nairobi in Kenya but operate in Sudan. They include the Sudanese Women's Voice for Peace (SWVP), the Widows, Orphans and the Disabled Rehabilitation Association of the New Sudan (WODRANS), the New Sudan Women's Federation (NSWF) and the Mundri Relief and Development Association (MRDA). The organizations work in the marginalized and war-affected areas of southern Sudan. Their Nairobi offices provide a necessary interface with the donor world and a base for advocacy. Organizations such as these are well placed to set an example of interethnic harmony and cooperation that will be the cornerstone for peace inside Sudan.

women in the military

Enlisted women of all military ranks who were interviewed cited equality and empowerment as reasons for joining the southern rebel forces. Some women have risen through the ranks to become officers. Women had a more prominent role in the fighting forces in the early days of the SPLA than they do now. The Girls Battalion for young women and girls was formed in 1984, but it has since been disbanded.[47] Since 1991 the role of women in active combat has been greatly reduced.[48]

Women in the military stand apart in women's forums. They are assertive, confident and voice their opinions clearly. They gesticulate with their hands in contrast to civilian women, who keep their hands in their laps. Some of those who are no longer in active combat have risen through the ranks of civil administration.

Mary Biba Philip, the Yambio county secretary, is in the military, and Constance Nako, a first lieutenant in the SPLA, is chairwoman of the Yambio Women's Association. Constance is married to the regional secretary of Equatoria.

The army is a good place for women to be equal with men. First I was a nurse. Then I became a teacher. Then I did a secretarial course. I wanted to join the army in Khartoum when I was a young girl. I admired the way they dress. When I got here, I was able to join. I wanted to fight with the men for our land. If I die, so be it. I will stay in the army even if there is peace. The army must still take care of the country. The battle to recapture Yei took place in 1997. Fifty women soldiers fought there. I'm one of the 50. We were very strong. A Toposa called Mary saved seven men by shooting [at the enemy with] a Bren gun during an ambush. We were very grateful to her. I am not nervous when I go into battle. I feel proud and happy. We are told not to think of dying. You think of how to defend yourself.

Constance Nako, Yambio, Western Equatoria

The pursuit of equality through enlisting can backfire, however. Women from most cultures in southern Sudan have a strong sense of the communal welfare of their group. They consider children and other vulnerable members of a community to be their collective responsibility. Civilian women safeguard their position in society by networking with their peers and take advantage of self-help and NGO-initiated projects. Women fighters who serve at the front miss out on the opportunity to create a social safety net. When they come out of the war zone, they find that domestic life has passed them by. As active service is no guarantee of a wage, men at the front rely on their wives to provide for the family. If a woman soldier does not have a family unit to look after things for her back home, there is no obvious means of support. Thus her position in society becomes more, rather than less, vulnerable.

Fawzia Wilson, 31, is such a case. She is on leave of absence in Yambio, Western Equatoria, and is virtually destitute. Her husband, a teacher, is dead as are her husband's relatives. She does not have a plot that she can till. Perhaps because of the temporary nature of her residence, she is not a member of a women's group credit scheme, which would allow her to start a small business. When she returns to the front, she says, there will be no one to care for her two small children. Her case was brought to the attention of the Yambio women's group. They agreed to help Fawzia by trying to find her 'a little job' at their resources centre and by writing a letter to the commissioner detailing her plight.

> *Men say women are lower than them. I wanted to be together with them and not let them put their feet on my head. I want to sit side by side in a chair and see what is happening. They can't say, 'You are just a woman.' My gun is my husband. I've been three times to the front line—Yei, Keya and Morobo. I was in the first batch after liberation in the area. I was taken for training when I was 22. When there is a lot of noise and people are falling around me, I want to go in to fight for the land. I even want to die so that history will say a woman died here for her country. This fighting at the front is how we have to shed blood. Otherwise, if prayer is strong it may succeed. Bashir in Khartoum does not want to talk so it is better to finish it by fighting.*
>
> Fawzia Wilson, Yambio, Western Equatoria

recommendations

- UN agencies, NGOs and local authorities should acknowledge that women who have responsible positions in the community will provide the foundations for peace-building. It is therefore essential to provide women with development assistance, even if it is done alongside emergency assistance and even if circumstances dictate that the assistance can only be small scale. Development resources should include materials, microcredit, technical know-how, and training in vocational skills, numeracy and literacy, and civic procedures.

- A fundamental policy for UN agencies, NGOs and local authorities should be to embrace the concept that women in crisis-prone areas, women in areas of relative stability, and displaced and refugee women should be equipped with vocational and civic skills that will help to rebuild their country after the conflict is over. Women and men alike in refugee camps should be allowed to sell the products of those skills on the commercial market to provide their families with a source of income. Displaced women should be provided with vocational training and resources for small-scale activities.

- To bolster woefully lacking protection for refugee women, UN agencies, NGOs and local authorities should recognize that refugees are subject to the laws of the host country and not to Sudanese customary law. In addition, all host countries should enact refugee laws that acknowledge and protect the rights of refugees if they do not yet have such legislation on their statutory books.

- Women in the military forces should be provided with the same demobilization packages as their male colleagues, including resettlement and training.

women as decision-makers 5

In a topsy-turvy world, tradition can be a comforting touchstone that implies that at least something is left of the familiar life that once was. This is why women seek to retain the best of the old ways while inventing coping strategies that are more fitting with contemporary times. The authorities in rebel-controlled areas, with the support of aid agencies, are participating in the gradual but promising evolution of cultural values from an authoritarian patriarchy to a more equitable gender balance. However, the gap between men and women cannot narrow until women become part of the decision-making process. And for this to happen, women must have the opportunity to associate and the ability to organize. This goal is easier to achieve in places of stability, where women have greater access to education, than in conflict-prone areas. And some avenues of implementation are easier to pursue than others.

Three decision-making structures run parallel to each other. They are political (SPLM and SPDF), economic (associations, cooperatives and women's groups) and traditional (clan, extended family and kinship ties). The SPLM administers areas under its control through a nascent bureaucracy. The different depart-ments of the adminstration come under state secretariats. Governors head the regions, which are subdivided into counties headed by commissioners. Associations, cooperatives and women's groups are formed at the grassroots in SPLM areas. Women's groups operate within the SPLM structure and have a relationship with the Secretariat for Women, Gender and Child Welfare that is yet to be sufficiently well defined. The political and economic structures are often symbiotic although this is not always the case. The traditional clan structures are least open to encouraging women to become decision-makers.

The SPLA/SPLM National Convention, held at Chukudum in 1994, was a watershed for civil society. For the first time, civilians were included in what had formerly been a de facto military administration. As a result, in recent years, issues of concern to the public such as taxation, representation and the provision of services have been discussed more openly in public forums. During the Chukudum convention the SPLM resolved to pursue the full liberation, development and empowerment of women. A policy of affirmative action was reiterated by the SPLM during the Conference on Civil Society and the Organization of the Civil Authority in 1996, during the law workshop of 1999 and in 2000 as contained in directives to SPLM organs of administration and in the terms of reference for a survey conducted on the status of women and children.[49]

Despite avowals made on paper, women's involvement with the SPLM is limited by a lack of contact with the regional authorities. Women's associations work only with the county commissioner, who has no power to initiate activities and no mandate to promote women's issues. A more credible option would be to establish direct lines of communication with the regional administration.

SPLM liberation councils plan to meet once a year to discuss development issues that affect the community. They operate from the homestead upwards and the majority of the council members are women. The County Congress meets biennially. About 1800 people attend, and 450 places are reserved for women. The delegates to regional congresses are drawn from the payam congresses. Similarly, delegates to the national congress are selected at the regional congresses.

Opportunities to participate in formulating development policy through the SPLM bureaucracy exist, although they are limited. Women have spoken out on topics that directly affect their domestic family life. For instance, mothers who were concerned about their daughters dropping out of school because of pregnancy called for a stricter observance of a law that provides for a two-year jail term and the payment of compensation for the rape of girls under 15. Women have also demanded to have clean water to reduce infant mortality while the female employees of NGOs have asked for the roads to be maintained.

In the rare instances when women have a woman official to whom they can voice their concerns, the outcome can be constructive, probably because women officials can empathize with women's concerns. The only woman to have been appointed as a county secretary by the SPLM is Mary Biba Philip, who serves in Yambio in Western Equatoria. At the time she assumed office, Yambio had neither a primary nor a secondary school for girls. When women voiced concern that their daughters were illiterate, Mary Biba took action and oversaw the rehabilitation of a disused school, which was put at the women's disposal. She also championed mothers who complained that their sons were still being forcibly conscripted into the military despite a recent SPLA ban on underage recruitment. She was effective in persuading the local SPLA commanders to observe the ban.

Because women believe that their empowerment is threatening to men, they choose to focus on practical issues such as water, food and education. Yet even though women have been historically responsible for water, sanitation and nutrition, they exercise limited authority in these sectors of the civil administration. Only two locations visited during the course of research for this book consulted with women about the provision of water and sanitation. In Akobo, women were responsible for keeping the town clean. In Mapel, women had a say in the location of wells as some were on the sanitation committee.

With the exception of traditional birth attendants, women are rarely involved in providing health services. At the Yambio hospital, for instance, only a few women are on the medical staff:

four certificated nurses, one auxiliary nurse, one assistant laboratory technician and one medical assistant. Several factors contribute to women's limited role in health administration. The high incidence of illiteracy among women has meant that few qualify for training as health workers. In Mading, women said they were reluctant to leave their home and family for long periods of training, particularly as there are no incentives as a reward for this hardship. In Narus, the health coordinator said that women were not enrolling in a sanitation course because their husbands did not think this socially acceptable.

There are examples of women who have broken through the glass ceiling to attain positions of authority: secretary of the county development committee, vice chairman of water supply. The SRRA has one female county secretary, Jasmin Samuel in Mundri, Western Equatoria. All Family Affairs coordinators are women, but they are not invited to important SRRA meetings or training workshops and their roles within SRRA are not clear.[50] In Equatoria, where women have served as chiefs in the past, a middle-aged woman who has not been to school has been selected as the chief for Nimule County. Elsewhere in Equatoria, a woman sits in the regional court and another in a payam court. And Mary Biba has provided the inspiring example of being appointed county secretary of Yambio. There is also a female administrator of Tonj County in Bahr el Ghazal. These steps are promising but not good enough. The civil authorities must encourage more than token representation of women where policy and law are being carried out.

WFP has organized a women's relief committee, and women work for UN agencies and local and international NGOs. For instance, half of UNICEF's hygiene promoters are women although less than 5% of their pump mechanics are women. However, these are exceptions rather than the rule. More commonly, empowerment is attained by learning vocational skills that give women entry to traditionally male realms such as carpentry, tailoring, bread baking and running of restaurants. In some areas of stability, women have also built resource centres that serve as the focal point for group activities such as adult literacy courses and skills training.

A handful of Sudanese women's NGOs—such as WODRANS, the Sudan Women's Voice for Peace and the New Sudan Women's Federation—actively promote women's inclusion in mainstream policy formulation. Under the umbrella of the New Sudan Indigenous NGOs (NESI) network, these organizations' objectives go beyond humanitarian assistance to include capacity building. NESI encourages local NGOs to develop strong working relationships with local authorities, to build a vigorous civil society.

Women say that association for economic purposes poses many challenges. Those who are members of agricultural cooperatives report they are invariably excluded from the decision-making process by their male colleagues. Women's groups that are formed to pursue income-generation and credit schemes would appear to be the answer to male competition, but these groups too have yet to fully appreciate the advantages of organizing along democratic lines.

Women from the Naangbimo Women's Group, Western Equatoria are members of a carpentry cooperative of 13 men and 18 women. The cooperative was started in 1996 with the assistance of an international NGO. It makes chairs that it sells to the NGO and to people in the nearby town. Responsibilities are mixed between the sexes, but only the men undertake the arduous and possibly dangerous task of walking to a distant forest to cut down the palm fronds that are used for weaving the chair seats.

In the past, women were in darkness. There was no one to show us what to do. Now women are able to come together to do things for themselves. Most of our men are at the front so we have to be creative to bring money for our children. There are no salaries so what we get from the gardens and the chairs gives us something to live on.

Assunta, chairwoman, Naangbimo Women's Group, Western Equatoria

Members of women's groups say they would like to be more conversant with the procedures for conducting meetings. Nor do they fully understand how to implement an electoral process that would underpin accountability and transparency. As a result, women elected to office hold tenure for extended periods of several years, which serves to entrench authority and decision-making among only a handful. Illiteracy is another factor that inhibits cooperation and association. Members of women's groups say that those who cannot read accounts are wary of those who are numerate. Illiterate people can feel especially vulnerable when confronted with books and figures they cannot understand. Members who have not been to school worry that their educated colleagues may be concealing some financial details from them. True or not, their fears would be allayed and a climate of trust and cooperation created if all members were numerate and literate.

Another reason women are slow to work in groups is the paucity of trained and experienced leaders. Despite the obvious leadership qualities of many of the unschooled members of women's groups, most women who are elected to the posts of chair, secretary and treasurer are school graduates and teachers or have risen through the ranks of the military. Others have married into the military by becoming commanders' wives. Certainly at those locations visited in this study, it appeared that the same small groups of women were selected again and again to attend courses and workshops both inside and outside Sudan. Some aid workers have estimated that the pool of women chosen by aid agencies and NGOs for further education is no more than three dozen. This reinforces the strengths of the few and fosters elitism.

It would better serve Sudanese women if many different women were to attend at least one workshop each. Women should be included who appear to be less capable as well as those who have already demonstrated their ability to learn and understand. The SRRA is aware of this problem and intends to organize leadership workshops where women can be groomed for positions of responsibility.

Women in camps for the internally displaced have the opportunity to acquire skills and engage in small businesses through the women's groups. However, the income-generating activities that depend on NGO support are not always sustainable when the NGOs leave the area. Refugee women, on the other hand, have proven to be one of the greatest resources of southern Sudan for disseminating knowledge. Returnees use skills and education acquired in exile to improve the lot of their communities. In almost all the locations visited, the women's groups had been founded by women who had learned how to organize a women's group while in a refugee camp. In Narus all the women interviewed who were working for NGOs had been refugees and had acquired skills that they were sharing with other women. In New Cush, women who had founded a women's group in an Ethiopian refugee camp established another women's group on their return home.

Yet even in refugee camps women encounter problems in organizing. Serafina is an Acholi woman with obvious leadership qualities. She fled Sudan to a refugee camp in Koboko in northern Uganda. There she became head of a women's group that was assisted with a credit scheme by an NGO. Soon after the scheme started functioning, the group was split up by the camp authorities and relocated to other camps. Serafina managed to revive the credit scheme among the few members who had been relocated with her. They used money earned from their small enterprises to put their daughters through the Ugandan educational system.

Then Ugandan rebels attacked the camp.

Serafina and her friends abandoned the businesses they had fought so hard to establish and sought comparative safety back in Sudan. They chose to settle in Yambio, Western Equatoria, a place that is foreign to their ethnic group. The young girls, who held the promise of becoming tomorrow's leaders until their mothers' source of income evaporated, were forced to drop out of school. Neither have Serafina and her colleagues been able to realize their true potential, despite their history of entrepreneurial initiative, because they do not have the extended family connections that would enable them to be chosen for workshops and training courses.

Women who have access to a functioning support system and to information technology have proved they can organize effectively. In 2001 a group of Nairobi-based refugee women lobbied to halt the import of Sudanese oil into Kenya. The women chose to lobby as concerned individuals so as not to risk politicizing the NGOs they worked for. 'As women, it was our obligation to speak out,' explained Awut Deng, one of the lead activists and a peace mobilizer for the New Sudan Council of Churches.[51] The women's advocacy strategy was pegged to a document they authored called 'Tears of Blood and Oil', which they distributed on email to local and international contacts. They called on the Ministry of Foreign Affairs and representatives of Talisman Energy Inc. and rallied the Kenyan Women's Political Caucus and an opposition member of parliament to their cause. High-profile church services in Kenya caught the attention of the national media. In the end, the well-orchestrated campaign was unsuccessful in achieving its aim of blocking Sudanese oil imports.

There is potential for information exchange between women who are urban refugees in Uganda and Kenya and those who are living inside Sudan and in refugee camps. Sudanese women based in Nairobi and Kampala, who are fluent in local languages and sensitive to local culture, would make excellent facilitators for workshops and seminars held in southern Sudan. Yet very few projects draw on the expertise of exiles. An organization that is in the vanguard of exporting knowledge back home is the New Sudan Women's Federation. NSWF has centres in Mapel, Thiet and Rumbek in Bahr el Ghazal, Bor in Upper Nile, and Yambio and Maridi in Western Equatoria. Its members train paralegals and trainers for adult education. They also conduct literacy and women's rights workshops.

NSWF members and other Sudanese women who are based in neighbouring countries face daunting logistics to achieve a transfer of knowledge into southern Sudan. Costly airfares must be built into the budget. And, the women argue, they need vehicles on the ground so that they can meet people who live outside the towns and villages. Without access to radio communication it is impossible to warn people of their arrival beforehand. So itineraries are kept on hold until they reach their destination. Sitouna Abdalla, chairwoman of the NSWF, suggests that NGOs pool resources to fund a communal radio network to transmit messages. The network would be used to organize events and schedules in advance of arrival and to cast the information net wider by relaying the proceedings of workshops to women's groups in other counties and regions. In this way, remote areas would no longer be sidelined in the learning process.

In contrast to the progress made through the civil administration, traditional structures remain a barrier to equality. Once a woman's children are grown, she should be allowed to take on a decision-making role. Women with this status can speak out in public forums, and younger women rely on them to articulate their messages. However, many elders and chiefs continue to bar women from participating in decisions that fundamentally affect their lives in the belief that this is strictly a male domain. This also holds true in refugee camps despite efforts by camp officials to empower women. In fact, some refugee men take advantage of their distance from the clan structure back home to pervert tradition to suit their own ends.

At Kakuma refugee camp, the Ugandan community elected women onto its community administrative committee for the first time in 1999. When a gender officer suggested that Dinka elders follow suit, they refused out of hand. At the behest of the UNHCR Kakuma suboffice, a woman sits on each of the (customary) bench courts, but their opinions are not taken into account even when the complainant is a woman.

Thus, living in war conditions has had mixed effects on women's ability to enter the mainstream of existing power structures. The breakdown of clan and extended family networks, which could otherwise oversee fair deliberations, as well as the presence of an authoritarian military culture inhibit women's ability to maximize their potential. This is offset by a groundswell of independent thinking led by women who are single heads of household. These women are stepping outside the restrictions placed on them by society to make choices that improve their own lives and those of their families. At the same time the constant setbacks and betrayals of war have eroded the capacity to trust and communicate.

These qualities need to be reawakened if the mobilization of women is to be a success. The way forward for women's groups and other forms of association supports the position commonly held by donors that participation through association is not an end in itself. True progress comes about only when transparency and accountability have taken root. For this to happen, women across the board must have equal access to equal education.

recommendations

- Women must be well represented in the legal, administrative and other decision-making systems to ensure that they are part of the process that formulates policy for civil society and to ensure equal access to equal benefits and resources across the board.
- Grassroots women's organizations should be allowed to operate independently of administrative structures to enhance benefits that could accrue from opportunities presented.
- Members of women's groups and associations should be trained in literacy and numeracy and also civic procedure and electoral processes to ensure transparency and accountability within their organizations and to give them the skills to challenge male-dominated cartels in the commercial marketplace.
- Donors should encourage and fund urban-based women's refugee organizations to share skills they have acquired with women inside Sudan.
- Local administrations should be encouraged to reintroduce the practice of appointing female chiefs.

the impact of war

sexual violence – refusing the hut

War frays and tears the social fabric of clan relationships and family bonds for many reasons: death, displacement, hunger, poverty, desperation, exhaustion, selfish motives and anarchy. One way this has been manifested is in a greater incidence of sexual violence. Displacement and death have torn apart the family structure, so that women, who traditionally are supposed to be protected and guided by men, find they have no one to turn to in times of need. Just as there is nowhere to redress atrocities so there is no one to settle marital disputes when the extended family is scattered. War economies, in which resources become scarce, tend to emphasize women as commodities rather than as people, reinforcing their historical role of being subjugated by men. During research for this book, women frequently stated, 'We want change, but we are afraid'. Women and young girls have universal rights that transcend the mores of their particular society and these rights must be honoured so they can be freed from sexual persecution. It is critical that women in southern Sudan and in refugee camps are empowered through awareness of their rights as women.

> *In war atrocities occur. Violence occurs. We as men have violated certain rights that women should enjoy. We don't defend it. We must commit ourselves to not repeating this.*
>
> Samson Kwaje, spokesperson for the SPLM, speech at the launch of
> Overcoming Gender Conflict and Bias, 31 October 2001

Traditionally, violence in the home was sanctioned only under extreme circumstances.[52] Now rape, forced and early marriage, abductions and domestic violence all are common. They threaten women's advancement. Sexual abuse injures women both physically and mentally. It has a serious effect on a woman's psychology, triggering chronic depression, feelings of worthlessness and suicidal tendencies. Women who have been subjected to violent acts, by strangers during a military attack or on an ongoing basis by someone they know, are deeply traumatized and can become, to a lesser or greater degree, dysfunctional. Talking about their experiences to sympathetic listeners in group sessions can help towards easing the pain that otherwise scars for life. Sexual abuse has a serious effect on a woman's health too. It increases the incidence of sexual diseases and HIV, unwanted pregnancies, illicit and dangerous abortions and a higher maternal death rate.

When I was 19, I gave birth to my firstborn, a son. Then after two days the murahaleen [nomadic militias] came to our village. Ten men raped me. I was in a bad condition. They left me while I didn't know myself. [She was unconscious.] It was very bad for me. Neighbours tried to carry me, but the murahaleen returned. People ran away, and I stayed with my child. They [the murahaleen] didn't see me. They started to burn the houses and took the goats. At that time it was very serious. I saw that my urine was passing. I couldn't help myself because my body was paralysed. When the people made sure the murahaleen had gone, they came back and took me away. That is when I last saw my home.

I tried to walk slowly slowly until my husband followed me in the bush and tried to take my baby away. He told me that I was dirty and would infect him [the baby]. I refused because it was so small. That's when he [the husband] knifed me. He stabbed me several times in the stomach. He left me there. He thought he had killed me. I walked here with other people who found me in the bushes. I was passing urine and blood. When I got here, a doctor gave me some medicine and it stopped. Even now [eight years later] I'm having problems with my stomach. It hurts. And my hips hurt when I walk. I haven't had treatment up to now.

Now I'm all right, and my husband can claim me back because he's paid his dowry. I hear he has a new wife at home. If my husband comes for me, I have to go even if he decides to slaughter me. Even my brothers-in-law are here, watching me. They want to take me back to Sudan. I don't know who can help me. I can't go back because I don't want to die. That's why I'm here. All these problems are because of war. Before, he couldn't have beaten me or taken my child. The family was staying together. His father and uncles, they would have persuaded him not to do this. But his parents were killed by a tank. His uncles were killed or ran away. We don't know where they are.

I want to thank you for taking me to a doctor.* Even if nothing more happens and I stay the same, now I am happy. You have helped me.

Woman, name withheld, who left Rumbek, Bahr el Ghazal,
in 1992 for Kakuma refugee camp, Kenya

While sexual violence certainly occurs in peacetime, the weakening of social structures has increased the magnitude of violence against women not only during fighting but also within the home. For instance, nearly 80% of women interviewed for a report on sexual violence said they had been beaten for refusing to have sex with their husbands.[53] Rape is a frequently used weapon of war designed to demoralize the enemy. Abducted women are systematically subjected to rape throughout their period of captivity. The abduction of women in refugee camps for the purpose of forced marriage back in Sudan is rife. Thus many young girls marry early, either voluntarily or at the suggestion of their parents, to escape this violence.

Because it is difficult to impose law and order where there is armed confrontation, crimes commonly go unpunished. This

---

* The doctor said Mary needed an ultrasound scan, a facility that was not available at the camp hospital.

cycle of impunity will be broken only when the perpetrators are regularly subjected to the due process of a formal judicial system and experience retribution. Every effort should be made to codify and enforce punishments that will act as a deterrent to sexual violence. A war crimes tribunal, necessary as it is, because of its inevitable time lag between commission and punishment is not an immediate solution. Men should be held accountable for their actions as they take place. Military discipline must be considerably strengthened and administrative penal codes vigorously applied in cases of sexual violence. In refugee situations, authorities should report all crimes against women to the police in the host country and allow justice to take its proper course.

Although abuse against women is widespread, it is taboo to speak openly on sex-related topics. And because of its hidden nature, humanitarian aid workers pay insufficient attention to sexual violence. Women are reluctant to discuss their experiences of sexual abuse either in groups or with aid workers, particularly if the perpetrators of the violence hold positions of authority or are of good standing in the community. Yet southern Sudanese women working as counsellors say that women will open up during workshops where no men are present. It is common for men to be present during group discussions on female issues. When this happens, women tend to answer by rote. Women are sometimes forbidden to speak to outsiders about their experiences.[54] When they do, they are censured and stigmatized by male members of the community. Victims of violence risk further assaults from their attackers, frequently husbands or husbands' relatives, to intimidate them into silence. Often women do not realize that their rights have been violated and simply view the offence as accepted cultural practice. For example, no one voiced the opinion that forced or early marriage is a form of sexual violence. When wife-beating was discussed, it was frequently put

Throwing the Stick Forward

UNICEF/OLS

Mary Biba is the only female SPLM county secretary. Among her most notable achievements as secretary are insisting that children not be recruited into the army and creating the Girls' Education Task Force to increase girls' literacy in Yambio County.

triggers chronic depression. It is also linked to serious health hazards. It causes pregnancies among girls whose bodies may not yet be fully developed and who are at greater risk of dying during childbirth than older women. Teenagers are more susceptible to the transmission of HIV and sexually transmitted diseases than mature women.

Scarce resources have served to push down the amount of bridewealth to a degree that people find shameful. The bridewealth for a Bor Dinka girl used to be 30 to 50 cows until rival Nuer militia stole most of the Dinka herds. Now it is 7 to 10 cows. The Twic Dinka have complained that at times they have had to marry their daughters for mosquito nets, money and dugouts. In 1991 and 1992, there were even marriage transactions where the currency was hippo meat.[60] In refugee camps, where the possession of cattle is forbidden, the marriage negotiations are sealed with the purchase of a cow or bull. In this way there is recognition that a bridewealth debt exists that will be paid in the future when there is peace.

Rape, forced marriage and early marriage are intertwined. A girl seeks protection from rape through early marriage. A girl who is forced into marriage with a much older man for whom she feels no affection can suffer rape in the marriage bed.

Before the war I lived in Malakal. In 1996, when fighting broke out in Malakal, we moved to Wau County. We were displaced to Rumbek. From Rumbek we moved to Gargar. I am tired of moving from place to place. We have lost all our cattle and personal property. If it were not for the war, I would have finished my education and got married at the proper age according to my choice. Instead I was married at 15. On our way here there were a lot of cases of rape. Rape is one of the frustrations that leads a girl to decide that instead of being raped by many people, it is better to get married to one person who can protect you. Some of the girls are not able to look after themselves when their

One day a man wanted to burn a woman's vagina because she had refused to have sex with him. He called a friend of his and they held her legs apart. One switched on a lighter and told her that either she has sex with them or they would burn her. Many women are taken by force. They call it gun marriage. When they marry you, it is for the children. Sometimes you hear girls and women refer to their husband as 'that thing'.

Imagine a man having a dormitory of nine wives. What kind of thing is this?'

Woman from Western Equatoria

In many places, particularly the crisis zones, changing marriage patterns are driven by insecurity and the scarcity of men and resources. Many women said they were more watchful over their daughters and did not allow them to go out on their own. However, prolonged parental protection may not be to the girls' advantage when they need to become assertive to survive the hostile environment. Pervasive sexual violence is a major reason why girls are getting married younger. One girl said that when she was 17, she married a man of over 60 to escape rape. Nuer girls customarily marry at 15 to 17, but Nuer girls in Mading said they were marrying as young as 13. Their parents wanted them to have someone who could protect them, they said. Because of the war-induced shortage of men, other girls marry young to make sure they catch a husband. There are economic reasons for early marriage, too. Girls say that climbing the social ladder through marrying well is the only possible exit from an impoverished home. There are examples of parents carrying out a kind of futures trading, particularly in times of famine, by betrothing girl babies to well-off men. In return, these men put down prepayments of food and bridewealth to help the family in their time of need.[59]

Early marriage is likely to lead to a lifetime of sexual and domestic subservience that lowers a woman's self-esteem and they disregard long-held beliefs and taboos about abstinence during lactation and menstruation.[55] A woman who questions the wisdom of her husband's expectations is likely to be severely beaten until she yields to his demands.

This sense of urgency all too often gets skewed into a sense of entitlement for sexual services both within and without the marriage. Women whose husbands had joined a rebel movement said that domestic violence had increased in the home. They attributed this to 'soldiers' short tempers', suspicions of adultery on the part of the wife while the husband was at the front and excessive consumption of alcohol.[56] The incidence of rape has also risen. Soldiers consider women who are widows or whose husbands are serving at the front to be easy prey. According to Nuer custom a woman can take a lover if her husband has been absent from home for more than five years. However, if a man marries another man's wife when the husband has been away for less than five years, it is considered adultery.[57]

Field research conducted by the New Sudan Women's Federation for a book on sexual violence during conflict revealed that some soldiers deliberately rape when transfer is imminent, knowing that they will escape punishment as they cannot be traced. The findings also indicated that several decades of conflict had given rise to a culture of lawlessness that inculcated in some young soldiers a code of violent behaviour towards civilians.[58] Women in Western Equatoria said that the majority of rapists were soldiers and that they were sent to the front before compensation could be claimed from the family. However, rape also occurred when 'outsiders', men who had been displaced, attacked local women. True or not, the point in both these instances is that it is not possible to follow through with the customary mechanism of negotiation, compensation and settlement when family members are absent or when the disputing parties do not adhere to the same ethnic code of conduct.

into the cultural context of 'discipline'. Women would benefit greatly from learning about their rights as women and discussing among themselves what they perceive those rights to be. This holds particularly true for women in areas of frequent conflict where atrocities are most likely to occur.

Anna Kima, a peace mobilizer who frequently counsels women in the course of her work, tells a story of exceptional brutality inflicted by a soldier on his wife at the beginning of 2001. Two opposing factions from the same ethnic group in Western Upper Nile were preparing for battle. With her husband's permission, a woman from one faction led a peace delegation of women to parley with the other faction. The women cooked a meal for their husbands' enemies and spent the day persuading them to lay down their arms and go home. The women's mission was successful. But on their return home, the husband of the leader of the delegation was seized by jealousy and suspicion over her day-long absence. In a fit of temper, he grabbed an iron from the coals and seared her private parts. She begged him to stop. 'If you must punish me, sear my head instead,' she cried. 'It is from my head that I was communicating with those men.'

Southern Sudan's military culture has certainly redefined the roles of the sexes in a way that widens the gap between women and men. Drastically high mortality rates from war and famine have endowed the act of procreation with a far greater importance than it held in peacetime. According to Jok Madut Jok, a southern Sudanese who has researched the link between militarization and sexual violence, war introduces the tenet that if it is the duty of men to defend the homeland, then it is the women who must oversee cultural survival by reproducing at an accelerated rate. Pregnancy has shifted from being a condition of individual choice to one of national obligation. Soldiers returning from the front fear that if they do not impregnate their wives while on leave, they may die before they get another chance to breed more children. So

UNICEF/OLS - Stevie Mann

Women participate actively in peace conferences to resolve conflicts among southern Sudanese tribes. The conferences have proven to the women that, although usually silent members of their communities, their voices can have influence in some situations.

Traditionally, building a house is considered men's work in southern Sudan. However, the absence of men has forced women to take on many of their husbands' previous responsibilities. They have found strength in their additional responsibilities, though sometimes the extra pressure seems overwhelming.

UNICEF/OLS · Stevie Mann

Few health centres in southern Sudan have rooms where medical personnel can hold meetings and few women nurses to discuss health issues. Consequently, nurses and community health workers may organize impromptu education sessions under trees. These are useful opportunities to share information about HIV/AIDS and other diseases.

UNICEF/OLS · Stevie Mann

The high number of single-parent households in southern Sudan means that older children often rear their younger siblings. This girl is taking care of her younger brother, perhaps because her mother has to work all day in the field to scrape together enough food for the family to eat.

Singing and dancing are significant parts of southern Sudanese life. Songs are important methods of passing cultural traditions and moral messages to children and adults.

These women built a small hotel in Rumbek Town using a loan from an NGO. Competition from similar businesses forced them to improve their services and add on a small bar.

Collecting water is done by women and girls. In some areas, they queue at waterpoints for hours before trudging home with a heavy clay pot, calabash or jerrycan on their heads.

Women must keep an eye on their children while they cook. Juggling multiple responsibilities leaves a woman no time for personal development.

These girls are among those fortunate enough to attend school. Sadly, the dropout rate for girls is high, leaving very few to complete primary 8, much less secondary school.

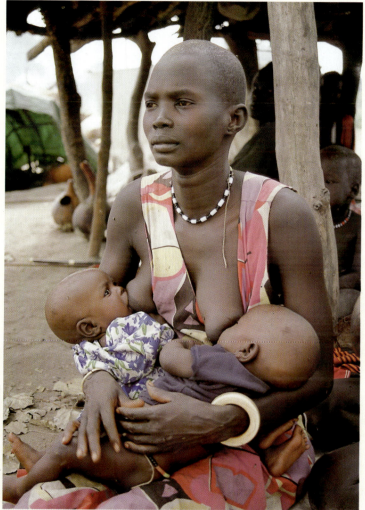

Breastfeeding is a source of critically important nutrients for infants, but many women in southern Sudan are too malnourished to feed their children adequately. This woman is lucky that she is able to breastfeed both her children.

UNICEF/OLS - Stevie Mann

More than 95% of the women are illiterate, which is a barrier to taking steps to improve their lives. The KonyRot women's group has initiated literacy classes using proceeds earned from catering UN and NGO workshops and from selling goods in the market.

UNICEF/OLS - Stevie Mann

parents lose everything; so the parents look for someone to support their daughters. If I had been in the town, I would not have got married. I got married because my family kept being displaced and people kept bothering them for girls. My parents said get married to this man so that he can protect you. Most girls in this area get married at the age of 13 and above. They are forced to marry, sometimes to a person they are not interested in and who is much older.

Young girl, Gargar, the sixth wife of the executive chief, who is in his 60s

The odds are stacked against a woman trapped in a violent marriage. From the onset, she encounters the premise that women must be disciplined, which implies that women are minors rather than equals. When violence occurs, her appeal process starts with her husband's family and continues through male-dominated customary courts. All these forums are prejudiced against her cause. Even her parents may harbour ulterior motives and encourage her to make the best of things. A daughter returned to the homestead means that bridewealth, disbursed throughout the girl's extended family, must be collected and returned to the estranged husband's family. Finally, a marriage ritual that sanctions wedlock to a stranger and physical assault to deflower the bride is hardly going to convince a young woman that her personal dignity and happiness count for much.

After the bridewealth has been given to the girl's relatives, a celebration is held, called 'mot'. When it is over, the newly wed girl and her escorts return to the home of the girl's parents. Her parents will have constructed a small luak [house] for her within their compound. She will eat with her parents but sleep in her own luak. After the newly wed girl has spent three days at her parents' home, her husband will come to secretly seek out his wife and give her new clothes and beads. From then on whenever she has her supper, her family will leave her alone. Every night the girl's husband will sneak into her luak and sleep with her until she becomes pregnant. When her first child begins to walk, she will go to her husband's home.

The first few nights there is a problem because the virgin bride is unlikely to easily accept her husband. It is expected that they will argue a bit and they may make noise. Sometimes the girl will tell her mother that her new husband has come and then she will climb into a tree and spend the night there. If this goes on for five nights, the newly wed man will go and tell his father-in-law that he thinks that his new wife does not want him. The girl's father will say to his son-in-law, 'It was the same with your mother. If your wife does not want you, she will tell me.' The newly wed man will keep trying to get the girl to sleep with him. If she keeps on resisting he will beat her and overcome her. If she screams no one will intercede because they know it is the usual way with newly wed girls.

Description of Nuer marriage ritual

In Nuer and similar cultures a woman can complain to her in-laws if her husband beats her. She first turns to a brother-in-law, who has the right to intervene if he is older than the husband but not if he is younger. If the beatings continue, the wife complains to her parents. The parents try to find out from both parties the reason for the beatings. If they think their daughter is misbehaving, they counsel her and send her back to her husband. If the woman's parents think that it is the son-in-law's fault, they tell him to take his cattle back and return their daughter. A husband is considered in the wrong if he beats his wife for sharing his food. Withholding food from other members of the family is a very serious transgression that can lead to divorce.

The conflict-induced shortage of men affects women even after their husband has died. According to the Dinka, bridewealth is given in exchange for a woman's fertility. A widow is inherited by her husband's brother or another male relative by whom she continues to conceive children who will bear the name of her deceased husband. This man is obliged to provide for the widow and all her children. He cannot dispose of family property without the widow's prior agreement. According to tradition, a widow has the right to choose the man who inherits her.

In crisis areas nearly every household has a widow—be she a grandmother, mother or sister. Widows are so numerous that they are straining the traditional coping mechanisms of wife inheritance. When there is not enough food to go around, men are doing the previously unthinkable. They no longer automatically provide for their dead brothers' wives and children. In response, widows find male protectors outside the patrilineal kinship group, a move that formerly would have been taboo. These resourceful women circumvent tradition with coping mechanisms that are acceptable to their deceased husbands' families. They make it clear that when the children reach an age of economic input they will be returned to the family. This particularly applies to girls, who will be exchanged for lucrative bridewealth after attaining puberty.

Traditionally the brother-in-law took the responsibility. Nowadays it is not the same. They make us pregnant, but they don't look after us. It's better to go to another man who is not a relative. Children always belong to the husband's family. It's frowned on to go outside the husband's family, but it is tolerated. My husband died, and I refused to be with my in-laws. Another man brought my children up. Later on, they were taken by my in-laws. I stopped giving birth because of the war. I had three children and was pregnant when my husband died. The relatives told me the brother would take over. In our tradition you wait a year. Then there is a ceremony where the brother takes over. I was given a brother-in-law. I stayed there two years, but he didn't help me at all. He already had a wife. I spent two years with no food. By that time, I decided to leave the house with the children and join another man. He was really polite and responsible and brought up the children.

> *All three were girls. One of them died. When the other two became*
> *mature [at about 16 or 17], the brother-in-law claimed them back. This*
> *is tradition so no one can quarrel with that. When they were married, I*
> *got my part of the bridewealth.*
>
> Mary Nyandio, chairwoman, Women's Association for Leech State

One way to safeguard the welfare of widows is to establish independent property rights for women within marriage. With so many female heads of household, it is critical that a woman's right to ownership is codified in the legal system and that local chiefs and elders are made aware of the legislation. If this does not happen, future generations of women are at great risk of becoming destitute. The interests of women will be well served when property issues and traditional marital practices are discussed at grass-roots community meetings.[61]

Finally, resource misallocation is a form of abuse against women that appears during times of war and famine. Women are responsible for food resources: cultivating, gathering food. It is they who queue to receive relief food at distribution centres. Yet they have little or no say as to the distribution of resources. For instance, a man may buy cattle with money earned by the wife and use those cattle as down payment for a second wife. The more wives a man takes and the greater the food deficit situation, the greater the risk of household resources being unfairly distributed among wives. It is often the most senior or the most junior wife who is discriminated against in this way.

the spread of HIV and AIDS awareness

The prevalence of HIV among the general population of southern Sudan is presumed to be much lower than in neighbouring eastern and central African countries. However, there are no statistics at all for the prevalence of HIV or AIDS let alone the incidence of HIV (percentage of the population that contracts the virus in any given year). What little information that is available indicates that women know very little about AIDS and are particularly at risk of being infected with HIV.

Statistics on HIV and AIDS are almost nonexistent and little sentinel surveillance has been done on HIV/AIDS despite increasing demands for such surveys.[62] The principle point of reference when discussing AIDS is a situation analysis consisting of HIV/AIDS/STD (sexually transmitted disease) knowledge, attitudes and practices that was carried out in the Equatoria towns of Chukudum, Juba, Maridi and Nimule in December 1997 and January 1998. At the same time, a HIV seroprevalence study was conducted in Chukudum, Juba and Maridi and in Malakal in Upper Nile. The survey was implemented through a UN agency in collaboration with SRRA in rebel-held areas and RASS and the Sudan National AIDS Programme in the government-controlled town of Malakal. It was the first time for both factions to collaborate on a humanitarian intervention. As the only study to look at attitudes and behaviour, it indicates that southern Sudan has yet to come to terms with the problem.[63]

Ignorance prevails regarding HIV/AIDS because reliable information that would indicate how it is spread simply does not exist. The list of unknowns is woefully long. There are no statistics on the prevalence of sexually transmitted diseases although STDs are one of the 10 most frequently reported ailments. Commercial sex is thought to be almost non-existent, but survival sex in return for food and other necessities is probably prevalent although communities do not talk about sexual practices. A rise in the incidence of tuberculosis is an indicator of greater HIV infection. Health workers have noted a rise in the number of drug-resistant tuberculosis cases among the general population, a standard indicator of greater HIV infection. Yet suspicions cannot be followed up as southern Sudan has only three machines for HIV testing, all of them at hospitals in Equatoria. Of course, without the means for testing, the UN recommendation of voluntary and confidential counselling and testing cannot be implemented.

On this foundation of ignorance, the spread of AIDS can either be halted or be allowed to become a firestorm that will eventually cut down hundreds of thousands of Sudanese in their prime. The classic ingredients for an AIDS epidemic are there: violence, poverty, oppression of women and girls, a poor health-delivery system, non-existent communications, very low school enrolment. There are others thrown in that are unique to certain African societies—polygamy, widow inheritance and female genital mutilation. Teenage marriage in polygamous circum-stances should also be included. Prepubescent girls up to around 14 are at greater risk of contracting HIV as their vaginal walls are not fully developed and battering from unwanted sex can cause dangerous abrasions. Female genital mutilation and STDs can also create tears and lesions. These too are opportunistic portals for HIV infection for both women and young girls. And finally, the overland supply routes for landlocked southern Sudan originate in countries where the HIV rate is known to be high. During the rainy seasons, truckers camp next to vehicles mired in the mud for days and even weeks during which time they seek sustenance and entertainment from the nearest little village. Trucking routes are one of the classic arteries for the spread of HIV from one African region to another.

The opportunity to prevent the deaths of hundreds of thousands of people 10 years from now is there. It calls for urgent and immediate interventions through education, awareness, condom distribution and surveillance.

Vowing to fight HIV/AIDS, in April 2001 the SPLM inaugurated the New Sudan National AIDS Council, a move that could go some way to dispel the silence and stigma surrounding the disease. This fledgling organization may be hived off from the SPLM's Health Commission and granted greater autonomy with membership to include NGOs and the churches. But by the end of the year, no programmes had been initiated, nor had women been singled out as a specific target group for education and prevention.[64]

Government-controlled areas come under the Sudan National AIDS Programme. SNAP runs HIV/AIDS awareness programmes in Khartoum and Gedaref in the north and in Juba in Equatoria. An organization that actively tackles the AIDS problem is the New Sudan Council of Churches. NSCC has inducted members of local communities in five Equatorian counties—Kajo Keji, Narus, Nimule, Yambio, Yei—in AIDS awareness. They include members of women's groups, soldiers, teachers and church leaders who talk about HIV and AIDS to women's groups, in schools and churches and other forums. By November 2001, NSCC had trained southern Sudan's first HIV/AIDS counsellors: nine people from Kajo Keji, Nimule and Yambio.

Meanwhile, leaders and educators, organizations and UN agencies working in southern Sudan or with southern Sudanese refugees need to ask probing questions. Which structures for AIDS awareness and education and for curbing the spread of HIV are not yet in place? Which need to be strengthened? Has a special curriculum on HIV/AIDS been integrated into the school system? Is there a special unit in educational departments to address girls' AIDS awareness? Expectant mothers are an ideal sentinel group for monitoring seroprevalence and the rate at which HIV is spreading. As this is the case, why is the equipment not available to test the routine blood samples taken in antenatal clinics? Is it possible to introduce programmes to prevent perinatal transmission of HIV? Are condoms freely available in towns and refugee camps? What mechanisms are in place for surveillance of sexually transmitted diseases?

It is a fallacy to think that AIDS will not reach epidemic proportions in southern Sudan just because it is at war and isolated from the rest of the region. HIV will spread rapidly through the population as there are no checks in place to stop it. Women will be particularly at risk because their sexual rights are habitually disregarded, leaving them virtually no escape from non-consensual and unprotected sex. Further, in many places 60% of families are headed by women. If the breadwinner dies, there will be no one to provide for the family. Southern Sudan cannot afford the luxury of delay. HIV infection and AIDS awareness must be taken very, very seriously today, not tomorrow.

Data collated during 1997–98 showed that married women, particularly those in their 20s, are at high risk of being infected with HIV, often through the risky behaviour of their husbands; 10% of the men engaged in casual sex but only 3.2% of the women. The majority of casual encounters were without con-doms. Nearly two-thirds of those in the control groups who tested positive for HIV were female. More than half of both men and women who tested positive were between 20 and 29 years old. The study found a significantly higher infection rate among women living in Juba. It also showed that over 20% of the infected group were housewives while only 2.4% were commercial sex workers and 8.7% were in the military. This is because very few respondents were soldiers or commercial sex workers. Over 40% of those who were positive said they were married. The study's findings on HIV seroprevalence was based on data collected in Chukudum and Maridi in Equatoria and the government-controlled towns of Juba and Malakal. The HIV seroprevalence ranged from 1% (Malakal) through 2.6% (Maridi), 3.3% (Juba) and 3.8% (Chukudum). Most of the study population were under 40, illiterate and highly mobile. More recently, 18.6% of blood donors screened for HIV at Yei Hospital in 1999 were found to be positive.[65]

The report demonstrated that women begin sexual activity at a younger age than men and that sex is conducted mainly within marriage. A very low percentage of girls (3.7%) engaged in sexual activity between 10 and 14 years, but the figure soared to 41.6% in the 15- to 19-year group as by that time about 45% of the girls were married. The statistics reflected that premarital sex existed in a small way among the girls. On the whole, however, they were more vulnerable to the risky behaviour of their male partners. Those interviewed for the survey were drawn from 10 different Nilotic and Bantu groups, all of which practise polygamy. Further, the frequency of intercourse indicated a vibrant sex life between husband and wife or regular partners. But only one in five had used a condom while engaging in casual sex. The majority of respondents said this was because condoms were difficult to find. Hospitals and family planning clinics were the principal providers of condoms, the study said. Informal findings show that very little is known of the hows and whys of using condoms and that many men view them with repugnance. One NGO said that it made condoms freely available at its health clinic, but that they lay gathering dust for an entire year.[66]

The study also analysed knowledge, attitudes and practices regarding HIV, AIDS and sexually transmitted diseases based on interviews conducted in the Equatorian towns of Chukudum, Juba, Maridi and Nimule. Overall awareness of AIDS was basic compared with that in neighbouring countries, the study found. And the women interviewed had less access to HIV/AIDS information and were far more ignorant of safe sex practices than the men. A good proportion of the control group thought that HIV could be transmitted by mosquitoes or by sitting on a public toilet. Half of the control group did not know about the use of condoms and nearly a third of the group knew about condoms but not where to find them. While one in five said they knew at least one person living with AIDS, two in five said there was no chance that they would become HIV positive themselves.

A study conducted in September 2000 by UNICEF for life skills education in and around Rumbek in Bahr el Ghazal and Yambio in Western Equatoria showed that AIDS awareness in the Yambio area was far greater than in the Rumbek area. The reason for this was not stated, but it is likely that awareness is generated by seeing people live with and die of the disease. The majority of adolescents interviewed by UNICEF in Rumbek, Bahr el Ghazal, were unaware of the dangers of sexually transmitted diseases even though they were in the most sexually active stage of their life. A few people living in payams outside Rumbek had heard of HIV and AIDS. However, few had ever seen a person living with AIDS or dying of it. In a society where illiteracy rates are high among people living in rural areas, 'seeing is believing'. This would imply that because the incidence of AIDS is probably low, there was no sense of urgency in learning about the ravages of the disease or about measures to prevent contracting it. Even so, youngsters in the Rumbek area expressed an interest in learning more about AIDS and HIV. Most of those interviewed in the Yambio area had heard of HIV/AIDS and wanted to learn more about it. Yambio is close to the border with the Democratic Republic of Congo, a country where it is highly prevalent. As a result, it is likely that cross-border travel has increased the incidence in Yambio.

A subsequent UNICEF survey conducted in 2000 confirms that awareness outside Equatoria remains low. According to the survey, about 75% of the people in Bahr el Ghazal and Jonglei had never heard of HIV/AIDS. This figure was marginally higher in Upper Nile (82%) and lower in Lakes (62%). This underlines the need for an intensive awareness campaign even though prevalence might still be low.

Risky behaviour compounded with other factors such as frequent population movements of refugees and displaced people, low standards of living, and difficulties in disseminating information through schools or health centres makes southern

Sudan very vulnerable to the spread of HIV. As with the rest of Africa, one of the arteries for the pandemic is trucking routes, which in this case are used to transport commercial goods and emergency humanitarian goods. Central African Republic, the Democratic Republic of Congo, Kenya and Uganda, the countries contiguous with Sudan's southern border, all have a high incidence of AIDS.

The survey shows that women urgently need a targeted intervention to reduce the spread of HIV as they are particularly vulnerable. One of the ways that HIV is contracted is by soldiers who have extramarital relationships at the front and then return home on leave determined to conceive more children with their wives. Another potential route of infection is through blood transfusions. Only three hospitals have the facility for screening blood for HIV. As anaemia is common and maternal mortality is high, the fortunate few who get medical attention may very well be at risk from tainted blood. Women are also at risk through rape, polygamy and wife inheritance. Further, girls are exposed to sexual activity at a younger age than boys, mainly through early marriage. Women and girls do not have equal access to information on HIV/AIDS. There are a number of reasons for this. Most women have not been to school and so are unable to read any educational literature that might be on display. Neither do they have easy access to the general flow of information as they tend to be sidelined from decision-making processes. Women will remain particularly vulnerable to HIV/AIDS as long as they are powerless over their sexual destiny. However, knowledge of how HIV is spread and practices that prevent the contraction of HIV would go some way to protecting women from this scourge.

Youth is another critical target group for HIV/AIDS education. The incidence of multiple partners and unprotected sex was higher among the younger age groups that UNICEF surveyed. This supports a case for interventions both at school and through family members. General education programmes are also badly needed. Risky behaviour had not been modified by changes in attitude at the time of the study. About 70% of those interviewed had had a sexual encounter with someone who was not a regular partner during the preceding month.

abductions

Conflict can be a hotbed for abductions. In southern Sudan, two very different types of abduction are practised. Interethnic abduction is a traditional weapon of war used to express rivalry and revenge. Fifteen years ago a different type of abduction emerged that continues to wreak untold psychological and emotional damage to the communities who are its victims. In this type of abduction, people are seized from their homes to be sold as chattels and forced to work against their will for no payment or reward.

The principal victims of this latter type of abduction are the Dinka living in Bahr el Ghazal along the fault line that divides the arabized peoples of the north and the Nilotic and Bantu peoples of the south. The perpetrators come from the Baggara, a cattle-owning, semi-nomadic, pastoral group who are arabized. Armed militias, known as murahaleen, travel on horses and camels or in vehicles, to cut a swathe of devastation through the countryside, pillaging and razing Dinka villages.

Until the end of 1985, the Dinka and the Baggara had enjoyed several decades of relative calm, derived from an agreement to share grazing grounds in times of plenty and of scarcity. Then localized drought that led to conflict over dwindling resources was exploited to trigger a resurgence of raids on Dinka villages. At first just a proxy force for destabilization, in 1989 the murahaleen were absorbed into the government army. Abductions continue to be executed frequently and with impunity to this day.[67] Villages in the counties of Western and Eastern Aweil and Twic in northern Bahr el Ghazal bear the brunt of successive waves of murahaleen attacks.

Abductions are intrinsically a gender-specific form of violence; women and their children are abducted, and men and the elderly are killed. As many as 14,000 Dinka women and children may be captive in Southern Darfur and Southern Kordofan. UNICEF estimates that 5,000 to 10,000 children have been seized since the onset of the war.[68] Once abducted, these women and children are deprived of all rights.

The murahaleen use teenage girls as concubines and for domestic labour. Older women are often sent to work in the fields. Women and girls alike are subjected to rape. Some are subjected to female genital mutilation, even though this is against Dinka custom, while others are forcibly converted to Islam.

About three years ago, Arab raiders kidnapped me. I had my four children with me, three girls and a boy. During the time I was captured I was treated very badly. Somebody tried to have sex with me, but I refused.* We had no freedom. Sometimes we spent two days without food. Because of the beatings I suffered, my teeth were broken, and I still have pains in my neck.

The first time I tried to escape, I was beaten very badly. They tore my upper lip, where you see this scar. When I did escape, I managed to take two of the children. If they had caught me the second time, they would have killed me. [When I got here] some people gave me clothes, others gave me pots and some gave me sorghum. I am happy now because I have returned to my people.

Akwal Bak, an escaped abductee

---

* The woman relating the story would almost certainly have been subjected to sexual assault on many occasions, and it is very unlikely that she would have been able to repel the attacks. The translator in this instance was a man. Women do not relate accounts of gender violence in front of men.

Some women who have escaped captivity speak of forming an unspoken bond with murahaleen wives. A favourite punishment of the murahaleen masters is to deprive the women of food and make them sleep outdoors. When this happened, the wives demonstrated solidarity by bringing the women plates of food behind the husbands' backs.[69]

For women, the trauma of witnessing brutal atrocities inflicted on their family and kin, which they are helpless to prevent, runs deep. Listening to survivors of raids relate what they saw, it is easy to understand why. Mothers watch helplessly as their children's heads are bashed in with a pestle that only the day before they would have been using to grind the family's grain. In one specific instance, five men followed the murahaleen in a bid to rescue their wives. The men were caught and, as the women watched, murahaleen cut off the men's arms at the elbow then moved on, leaving them to die.[70]

> If a boy tries to escape and is caught, his legs are cut off with a knife. If he resists having his legs cut off, his hands are tied together and he is dragged behind a pickup until he dies. Boys who have their legs cut off herd camels. They are tied onto a camel in the morning and untied at night. They are given a girl [abductee] to make children.
>
> Johannes Bul Garang, taken from Aweil, Bahr el Ghazal,
> in captivity from age 3 to 15

Women who survive the terrors of captivity to return home are not stigmatized. Neither are their children conceived with a murahaleen master. Communities are overjoyed when abductees return home and make an effort to reintegrate them into daily life. They may at first encourage them to talk of their experiences, but then the women are advised to forget about the past and look forward. These women marry, fetching less bridewealth than other wives because they are 'second hand'. Their half-Arab children are either embraced by the husband and take his name or are taken into the family of the woman's father and assume their grandfather's name. If the new husband agrees to take them into the family, he will give six cows for a son and five cows for a daughter.[71]

> I was coming from Aweil with my family—my mother and father and brothers and sisters. We met murahaleen along the way and they started shooting people. We tried to hide, but we didn't know what was happening so we sat down. Then six murahaleen came and started shooting us. They shot me through the cheek and in the arm and in the leg. They stabbed my mother and took my sister, the one who follows me. When they took my little brother, he jumped off the horse and they knifed him. When this happened, we all got separated. I walked with my other small brother for three days without food. We saw no one. When we passed, people hid in case we were murahaleen. Then I saw some people. I put my hands up to show I was not murahaleen. They took us to their place in the bush and washed my wounds and gave us something to eat.
>
> Mary Atong, 12, Gogrial, Bahr el Ghazal

In April 1999 and April 2000 the UN Commission on Human Rights adopted resolutions expressing concern about abductions and forced labour in Sudan. In May 1999 the Sudanese government established a Committee for the Eradication of the Abduction of Women and Children (CEAWC), which works closely with UNICEF. In January 2002, President Omar Hassan Ahmed El-Beshir strengthened the committee by transferring it from the Justice ministry to his own office.

The southern tribes also steal each other's women and children when at war with one another. Such abductions are a long-standing method of revenge in the ethnic rivalries of southern Sudan. Tribe-on-tribe fighting involves stealing both people and animals. The objective is to weaken the enemy while at the same time strengthening the size and gene pool of the victors, through abduction, and increasing the herds of livestock, through cattle rustling.

Thus abductees are thoroughly assimilated into the ethnic group that has captured them. Women and children almost always enjoy the same rights and status as any other member of that group. The male abductees can even aspire to leadership within their adoptive ethnic group when they grow up. However, despite being put on an equal footing with their captors, abductees are robbed of their native culture and language, even their birth names. This is a violation of human rights, especially of children's rights. While this book was being researched, interethnic child abductions were reported in locations in Eastern Equatoria and Upper Nile. The Dinka, Murle and Nuer are some of the tribes that abduct women and children.

In Akobo in Jonglei, wives said they were dismayed that their husbands had flouted their wishes and returned with a war booty of captured children after a battle with the Murle. They were also concerned that their own children continued to be abducted by men from other ethnic groups. The women expressed a strong desire to break the cycle of child abduction, which affected them as much as it did their traditional enemies.

trauma

It is crucial to the rehabilitation of civil society to address trauma, the hidden legacy of war. Sudanese women have shown themselves to be astoundingly resilient in the midst of miserable and dangerous conditions, exhibiting none of the self-pity that would prey on Europeans and Americans under similar circumstances. If anything, the outsider would characterize women from southern Sudan as impassive. This is far from the truth. The calm exterior masks tumultuous inner feelings. Sudanese women remain silent, believing that expressing their feelings may threaten their own ability to survive. This is particularly true for women from Nilotic ethnic groups. Women from Bantu ethnic groups such as the Azande seem to find it easier to share sorrow.[72]

There have been no investigations into the psychological well-being of southern Sudanese women, but mental health assessments of refugee and formerly abducted girls in their late teens reveal strong evidence of ongoing post-traumatic stress disorder (PTSD). In fact, the abducted girls had witnessed and experienced such horrific things that the normal Western-style stress parameters drawn up for the interviews simply did not apply.[73]

The severity of wars, based on disaster medicine, is measured through death rates and number of people injured while the mental health consequences of war—violence on shattered minds—is invisible. Mental health care in war-torn societies is more complicated than rebuilding roads or treating malaria, but of equal importance.

Richard Mollica, Scientific American, June 2000, p. 3639

The vast majority of war-affected people are physically and emotionally exhausted, despairing and mistrustful. They experience low-intensity but long-lasting problems related to mental health—chronic and severe depression and PTSD—rather than mental illness such as schizophrenia and psychosis. Manifestations are feelings of anxiety, depression, guilt and helplessness. In southern Sudan emotions are intense because of the particularly brutal nature of the atrocities committed and the state of perpetual insecurity in which people live. Most people have been under threat of attack or displacement for nearly two decades.

Research conducted on the psychosocial functioning of 137 boys and girls in areas of instability showed that four out of five had witnessed people being killed and almost as many had seen huts burning. All but 4% of these children had been caught up in an attack by armed men. Young women interviewed by mental health professionals spoke of being in the midst of chronic and extreme violence as witnesses and victims. For instance, a 13-year-old girl who had escaped from her murahaleen masters watched as someone was tied up, thrown onto the ground and beheaded with a panga (machete). Abducted youngsters who had managed to escape captivity said they feared bombs, attacks, hunger, disease and being alone. Refugee girls who lived with foster families displayed symptoms of trauma, depression, anxiety and hopelessness. Some were prevented from becoming suicidal only through their religious beliefs. They longed for security and education, which they equated as being synonymous. They were frightened of being trapped in an arranged marriage.[74]

> When the war came to Bentiu, Rebecca was living with her parents and brother. They all ran away together but her father died while they were running. He coughed blood and died. As they continued to flee, she got separated from her mother and brother and later people told her that her mother had died. She does not know about her brother. After she lost her mother she ran with other refugees but not anyone she was related to. When people caught some small animals they gave her some meat so she was able to stay alive. She continued to follow those people but she was very small and could not keep up. That was when she was raped by an old man. She was crying and screaming so other people came and chased him away. She was very sick and vomiting and in great pain then. She still has internal pain from the rape and fears that she may be so injured that she will not be able to have children.
>
> Eventually . . . she met Agnes, an older lady who claimed to know

Rebecca's parents. Agnes asked her to come to live with her so Rebecca agreed. They entered Kakuma [refugee camp] in 1993. At that time Agnes was a widow with two children. She now has four. For the first three years, Agnes was kind to her and allowed her to attend school. For the last five years she has been increasingly cruel, beating her frequently and making her do all the work of the house. Sometimes Agnes is angry with her and tells her to leave the house and never return. Rebecca has nowhere else to go so she stays and tries to comply with the woman's requests.

Now it is worse because Agnes wants her to marry. Instead, Rebecca wants to become educated so she won't have to depend on cruel people. But she is now prohibited from attending school. If she goes, the lady sends one of her children to get her and she is beaten severely when she gets home. When neighbours intervene, Agnes says, 'I feed her and she does not do what I tell her.' Sometimes she sneaks out to go to school but she cannot really learn because she does not go often enough. She feels desperate about her lack of schooling because she believes that her only chance of a safe life is to be educated and self-sufficient. Rebecca attends St Peter's Catholic church and finds great solace in her religion. She hopes God will guide her to a better life and therefore she has the courage to endure for the present.

> *A composite story with changed names from Best-Interest Assessment Interviews for orphaned girls of 16 and 17, Kakuma refugee camp, Kenya*

Julianne Duncan, a psychosocial worker at Kakuma refugee camp who in 1999 and 2000 assessed unaccompanied boys and some unaccompanied girls like Rebecca for the purpose of resettling them permanently in another country, concluded that of 174 children interviewed, 168 were suffering from symptoms of unresolved trauma. In other words, they were living in a traumatic present and did not believe that the refugee camp was a safe place. The youngsters were not delinquent and did not have memory disorders. A large proportion of the group suffered from anxiety. While the boys expressed grief and sadness, the girls tended to exhibit symptoms of depression, possibly because they felt they had no control over the outcome of their lives. Duncan surmised there was a greater sense of hopelessness among the girls because they felt their future was doomed. The girls expected to be dispatched to a stranger in a forced marriage and entertained little hope of being given the chance of a future life in a new country. To a large extent, their predictions came true. As it turned out, the ratio of boys to girls who were resettled was disproportionate even given the far greater number of boys living in the camp.[75]

It is likely that many women in southern Sudan are also suffering from ongoing and unresolved trauma. They are exposed persistently and unpredictably to the things they fear such as soldiers and guns. Worse, the government is waging psychological warfare against southerners through aerial bombing campaigns, which have intensified in recent years. In 2000 nearly 100 civilians were killed by bombs, according to figures compiled by NGOs operating in the south. The bombs hit homes, schools, churches, hospitals and marketplaces. Some were 55-gallon drums packed with dynamite and nails, designed to cause maximum destruction with exploding shrapnel. Virtually all women interviewed for this book had been subjected to bombing raids. Others said they had frequent nightmares about being bombed.

I [dreamed I] was running from a plane that was flying above us. An Antonov. When it landed a small girl who looked like an Arab stepped out and started walking towards me. There was liquid like oil that is burning where it touches you. You have to die if the bomb touches you. It fell on a woman and we took her to the river to put her in the water. I was frightened because the plane was coming, and it was going to drop a very bad bomb. I don't know why I dreamed of an

Arab girl. Maybe she wanted to come to make friends, but now we are scared of Arabs because of the bombs. If it was just women, we could talk to the Arabs and there would be a chance to have peace in the country.

Serafina, relating her dream, Yambio, Western Equatoria

Trauma can leave an invisible signature on a person's behaviour. Anxiety, depression and PTSD are triggered by visible cues, such as an Antonov bomber flying overhead, or the memory of traumatic events such as elderly parents being consumed by flames inside a blazing hut. However, populations living in war zones adapt to trauma and develop a far higher stress threshold than those living in peaceful areas. This means they are resilient to what is known in the West as nervous breakdowns. It has been found that the majority of people in countries such as Sudan continue to function in their everyday lives and can make a full psychosocial recovery. The fact that populations on whom war has had an impact can survive with little or no professional assistance suggests that the most effective route to recovery from trauma is an amalgam of counselling for groups and individuals and more practical self-help interventions such as providing materials with which the women can earn some money, so that they can regain control of their lives.[76]

I met women in Mapel who had been displaced by fighting. One woman had lost five children. The first time I talked to her, she could only cry. She returned in the evening and explained how it had happened. She had a son and four daughters. The son was put in the mortar and his head pounded while they watched. The daughters screamed but the mother couldn't find her voice and was silent. They fled on foot and the four girls slowly died of hunger, one after the other, day after day. I told her, 'You still have a child. You must take care of it and have hope.' The next morning the woman returned

113

smiling and speaking, but it was too much for me. I didn't feel well that day.

Awut Deng, peace mobilizer, New Sudan Council of Churches

Places that are bombed regularly, such as Yei in Western Equatoria, disrupt lives to the point where people begin to regard investment in the future as futile. They do not rebuild houses as they could be bombed again the next day. And they wonder why they should bother planting crops when there is every chance they will be destroyed before the harvest.

Development interventions in education, health and micro enterprise restore hope and dignity as well as encourage rehabilitation. Women say they do not want to be perceived as victims but as useful human beings whose skills should be developed and put to productive use. A woman who contributes to her own livelihood has taken charge of her destiny. This empowerment is vital for the healing process. For instance, women feel demeaned when they queue for relief rations at distribution centres. They would prefer a food-for-work scheme, they say. Thus in several ways, development programmes are as crucial to crisis-prone areas as they are to areas of relative stability.

Stress levels are reduced when people have control over their surroundings and can predict events. In war zones, of course, this is not the reality. The other option to diminish stress and PTSD is catharsis through expression. In literate societies, this could be through writing down an account of the traumatic experience. Counsellors for refugee victims of torture organize evenings where their clients cook national dishes to share among themselves, an act that soothes yearnings for the past and creates new bonds of friendship. In southern Sudan, where women are largely unschooled and food is often scarce, alternative solutions for restoring mental health must be found.

Abducted children who have escaped from captivity cope with

stressful memories by talking and dancing through the night. Children who were asked to relate their experiences at the hands of the murahaleen broke into song when the memories became too painful.[77] All these are effective psychological interventions that women could adapt. Peer support and interaction could be achieved by bringing women together, with a trained counsellor in attendance, to talk of their experiences and express their fears through song and by relating their dreams.

Elsewhere in Africa, such as in Uganda, women have been brought together to relate before other women the atrocities that have been committed against them. They deliver their testimonies in their mother tongues and are encouraged to relive their suffering in every detail. These confessions are made in a safe environment before an attentive and non-critical audience of women. The process of interaction between the protagonist and the audience is a statement of cultural acceptance and exoneration of the victim's part in the crime that has been committed.[78] Delegates to the people-to-people peace conferences in southern Sudan, who shared stories of the horrors they had survived, experienced a similar catharsis. Western psychology uses parallel healing processes. The re-enactment of traumatic events provides opportunities to exorcise bitter feelings and vent repressed anger.

> *I don't know what you have done to me. I have stood up and spoken in front of a crowd. I have never done that before. Now I feel my legs are strong enough to stand.*
>
> *Payam administrator, Tonj County, Bahr el Ghazal*

Horrific experiences stir up feelings of grief at the loss of loved ones and anger at the injustice of the atrocity or violence that has taken place. When their socio-cultural structures collapse, survivors begin to question their identity. They also yearn to be safe and some seek solace through religious faith.[79] Outside intervention is possible to various degrees. Conflict-resolution workshops and peace conferences are in themselves a healing process, even before the outcome of what has been learned and discussed becomes clear. Human rights abuses that go unpunished engender anger, frustration and distrust of others. A community harbouring these negative attitudes is not ideal material for cooperative action such as is called for in women's groups. Workshops on rights and gender awareness and the proliferation of paralegals would help to resurrect community identity and cohesion. Some human rights are safeguarded in the civil administration's legal system. It is important that local chiefs, elders, women and other community members are made aware of the legislation and that justice is seen to be done to provide a deterrent against future crimes.

recommendations

- To break the existing culture of impunity, the military and administrative legal systems of all warring parties must be strengthened to ensure that those who commit crimes against women and girls are brought to trial immediately.
- The welfare of widows and single heads of household should be safeguarded by codifying women's independent property rights within marriage in both administrative penal codes and customary laws.
- UN agencies, NGOs and civil administrations must implement urgent and immediate interventions to slow down the spread of HIV/AIDS through education, awareness, condom distribution and surveillance.
- Women should be able to ease the trauma inflicted by acts of war committed against themselves, their family and their

116

community by having access to counselling. Women who have been subjected to rape and other sexual violence must have access to medical treatment.

conflict resolution

7

I shall reconcile you
Even if it's a quarrel between husband and wife,
Even if it's between brother and sister,
Even if it's between two villages,
I shall reconcile you.
sung by Awut Deng, peace mobilizer, at the Wunlit Conference

Few southern Sudanese can hear the drone of an approaching airplane without a twinge of apprehension that it might drop a bomb. They cannot remember when the able-bodied were not conscripted into the military or what it is like to walk without fear of treading on a landmine. Planning a future in ancestral homelands, secure in the knowledge that development will benefit the clan for generations to come, is a concept beyond understanding. Two phases of a civil war that has spanned almost half a century with no resolution in sight have pushed the coping strategies of the southern Sudanese to the edge. They would do anything in their power to negotiate a just conclusion to the violence.

War is like a juggernaut, exacting sacrifice from the individual for the supposed good of the many. Invariably in low-tech, drawn-out fighting, women bear the brunt. They are killed, raped, looted, abandoned and displaced. They go hungry and have no means of support. Their claim to respect and protection within the clan and the family is stripped from them. In short, women and their children are the true victims of war.

We get up and pray when we have bad dreams. We pray that there will be peace. We don't want revenge. When there is war, your inner

feelings are always inwards [worrying about survival]. When you are
sleeping that feeling is there.

Mary Nyandio, Nyal, Upper Nile

To stereotype women as peacemakers is misleading just as it
would be wrong to say that all men want to pursue war. Women
have signed up to fight while others help behind the lines. During
the SPLA assault on Gogrial town, Bahr el Ghazal, in June 2000,
the troops were sustained by local women who brought cooked
food and milk to the trenches from as far as 60 kilometres away.
They often risked bullets and mortars to reach the soldiers. This
support emboldened the fighters to such an extent that they
overran the town sooner than expected.

Traditionally, however, women were non-partisan medics on
the battlefield and mediators behind the lines. They followed
their men on raiding parties so that they could treat the wounded
from both sides, even hiding and saving the lives of enemy
casualties. Before this war, the women say, men listened when they
said the fighting had gone on long enough and must stop. Now
women have no voice in these matters. They are told of the dead
who have fallen in battle and weep for the wasted lives of their sons
and husbands.

Women are fed up with the war. They don't even know why it's going
on. They are always asking the men to stop it. The women are coming
out and talking. They have even stood up and said they won't bear any
more sons if they are going to be sent to the front line.

Elizabeth Otieno, New Sudan Council of Churches

The atrocities that occur in contemporary interfactional
fighting violate traditional warfare practices. The Dinka and Nuer
used to fight with clubs and rarely killed each other. If a combatant
died, spears were introduced and the conflict escalated. Disputes

were usually over grazing and fishing rights or over the abduction or impregnation of girls. Traditionally peace was restored by means of discussion, negotiation and compensation through the mediation of acknowledged leaders of the kin groups involved. For instance, a death that occurs during a Nuer battle carries compensation of 50 head of cattle. A fine paid in cattle and imprisonment for three to six years may also be imposed depending on the circumstances.[80] Among the Avokaya, Baka, Moro, Mundu and Zande of Western Equatoria a truce can be sealed with a symbolic exchange of each other's blood. Dinka women contribute to the ritual of reconciliation by bringing the men calabashes of water to wash their hands as a metaphor for washing away past disagreements. Traditional mediation mechanisms helped to reinforce interclan and clan support and cooperation in the wake of disputes.

The complicated dynamics of this war that pits not only northerner against southerner but also southern ethnic groups and even clans against each other has overwhelmed traditional methods of conflict management and resolution. The credibility of elders has waned over the years as their ability to prevent conflagration proves useless against the power play of local military commanders. Women have stepped into this void and are drawing on the positive aspects of their traditional role as peacemakers to rebuild their communities. In Narus, the communal Justice and Peace Committee was born out of the local Sudanese Women's Voice for Peace chapters. In Akobo and Mading, the women asked Riek Machar to issue decrees that resulted in a cessation of hostilities and the prohibition of shooting, for a short time.

> *We would like peace but do not have the power to bring it. You have to start at home with the way you stay with your neighbours. You have to teach your neighbours how to stay with each other, forgive each other.*

Every fortnight all the women's groups meet as women to discuss our problems. Many women come. The Didinga in the hills are treated as if they are separate from us. We would like to have unity with them. Currently they are causing insecurity. They attack people on the road to Chukudum. They attack vehicles. Sometimes they loot. If you resist them, they kill you. We would like to talk to them so that there is freedom of movement in the area. The major hospital is in Chukudum. This insecurity causes great problems because we cannot take children to hospital.

Eastern Equatoria Women's Group, New Cush

Women are valuable mediators in disputes between different lineages because of their dual affiliation through marriage. Even in patrilineal societies, matrilineal links to other clans are important instruments for peacemaking. Women are enthusiastic participants in peace movements and conferences as well because in many ways war exacts a higher toll from women than men. This holds true even in the military as can be seen from the experiences of women soldiers. While fighting at the front they take on the duties of a man without abandoning the responsibilities of a woman. This theory is borne out by the case history of Fawzia Wilson, who was interviewed (see under 'Military' in chapter 4), in Yambio, Western Equatoria. There was no one to look after her children while she was serving in the ranks of the SPLA, and she had no means of supporting them when she came home on leave. Conflict undermines cultural roles and renders women the breadwinners on whom the survival of the family depends. So peace holds a different promise for women than it might for men, whose wartime obligation is fulfilled at the frontline.

As often happens, the people of southern Sudan have turned to religion to provide a healing touchstone in a turbulent world. A resurgence of culturally acceptable conflict-resolution methods has taken place under the auspices of the New Sudan Council of

Churches. The NSCC initiative seeks a united southern Sudan by working with southern Sudanese ethnic groups at war with each other. Their constituency is the chiefs, clan elders, women and youth. The objectives of the NSCC peace-building campaign are to cease localized hostilities and violations against civilians, to return abducted women and children to their families, to introduce an amnesty on past hostilities, to create equitable sharing of border grazing lands and fishing grounds, and to encourage freedom of passage, trade and communications across common borders. Longer-term goals are the repatriation of the displaced to their communities, good governance under the auspices of responsible leadership, and provision of essential services such as water, sanitation, schools and health facilities for people who have returned to their home areas.

The first meeting of warring ethnic groups, the Nuer and Dinka, convened at the Kenyan border town of Lokichoggio in June 1998. This all-male gathering of 35 chiefs and church leaders signed an agreement to cease hostilities and allow freedom of movement between Dinka and Nuer areas. The initiative was successful enough to justify a larger gathering the following March in the Dinka constituency of Wunlit, Bahr el Ghazal, on the west bank of the Nile. The delegates signed a peace agreement that ended eight years of abduction of women and children, large-scale cattle rustling and destruction of villages. Over one-third of the signatories were Dinka and Nuer women.

Wunlit drew grassroots representation from nearly every Dinka and Nuer area. One-third of these delegates were women. Participants sat beneath shady trees and listened as each side spent a full day venting its grievances and anger. Issues such as abduction and peacekeeping along common borders were staked out and assigned to working groups. The groups' final proposals were put to the vote at the closing plenary session.

It is not enough that women have a voice in conflict resolution.

They must also be part of its implementation. This was the case at Wunlit, where they were deeply involved in all aspects of the peace process. Women sat on the peace-monitoring committee that ensured no fighting took place during the conference. They were on the mobilization committee that explained the conference objectives at grassroots level. They helped trace abducted children and return them to their families. Wunlit was a milestone for southern Sudanese women. It adopted a principle of affirmative action to ensure that women were fairly represented in decision-making. As a result, delegates set clear targets that addressed women's concerns about human rights violations. Wunlit's other great achievement was that it sowed the seeds for empowering civil society.

> When we were brought together, all the bad things we held within us were aired and brought to the fore. When you have the opportunity to speak out your negative attitudes, it allows for something new to happen. Before we were looking with our eyes in two directions. But now we are able to turn our eyes in the same direction.
> Monika Ayen Maguet, delegate to Wunlit Peace Conference

In the aftermath of Wunlit, displaced Dinka and Nuer declared their desire to return to the abandoned border villages where the two ethnic groups once lived side by side. This has already begun to happen to the north of Rumbek in Maper, Bahr el Ghazal. However, a full-scale return programme is not feasible until donors underwrite the rehabilitation of infrastructure—roads, water and sanitation, schools and health clinics. Even so, the benefits of Wunlit are plain to see. In 1999 and 2000, government troops carried out a series of brutal attacks on Nuer villages in the vicinity of Lundin Oil of Sweden's drilling activities. Thanks to the Wunlit ceasefire, tens of thousands of displaced Nuer were able to seek refuge in Dinka territory.[81]

Trade between the Dinka and the Nuer flourished. When floods in 2000 caused famine in the Nuer villages of Nyal and Ganyiel, residents moved to the Dinka town of Yirol to barter their livestock for the Dinkas' surplus grain harvest. The free movement of people and goods continued to benefit both communities until early 2001 when the differing objectives of local military commanders reignited fighting between Nuer factions as well as between the Dinka and the Nuer. This interfactional and interethnic fighting threatened to unravel the Wunlit agreement, but it held firm. Outraged by the damage inflicted on civilians on the orders of military commanders, members of the West Bank Peace Council gathered at Ganyiel in Western Upper Nile in April 2001 to reaffirm the principles and intent of Wunlit.

These earlier initiatives to reconcile the Dinka and the Nuer evolved into a people-to-people peace process that embraced other regions and ethnic groups. The warring Lou Nuer met in Waat in November 1999, albeit with less success, as some of the factions were being armed by the Sudanese government. Anyuak, Dinka, Jie, Kachipo, Murle and Nuer drew up a covenant of peace and reconciliation at Liliir in Upper Nile in May 2000. The following year saw a series of mini-conferences for the ethnic groups of Upper Nile carrying on the Liliir recommendations. In the aftermath of a February 1999 ceasefire, the NSCC has attempted on several occasions to calm ongoing friction between SPLA troops and Didinga civilians at the SPLA garrison town of Chukudum in Eastern Equatoria. The limited success of this mediation indicates, not surprisingly, that civilians have greater faith in mediation than do the military.

Two other peace processes continue parallel to the efforts of church leaders and civil society. Women do not play a significant part in either process. One is the Intergovernmental Authority on Development (IGAD), representing Horn of Africa states, which has been ongoing since 1994. IGAD deals exclusively with the Sudanese government and the SPLA. Its declaration of principles enshrines the separation of religion and state and the right to self-determination. Women's groups and Christian and Muslim leaders have been urging IGAD to include them in the dialogue but to no avail. A joint peace initiative introduced by Egypt and Libya in 1998 seeks to include all northern and southern opposition parties and movements in reconciliation. The nine-point peace plan calls for an end to hostilities, after which a caretaker government drawn from all political entities will oversee the run-up to general elections. In recognition of the religious, racial and cultural diversity of the Sudanese people, it calls for a decentralized government but not for secession of the south. These initiatives address democracy, human rights, self-determination, and the separation of religion and state. But neither recognizes that oil exploration and drilling activities in the south are integral to the causes of the war and the solution to it.

Despite the successes achieved by the NSCC, donors have been slow to fund grassroots mediation and to recognize the importance of including women in the peacemaking process. This lack of material support inhibits the potential for reconciliation to take root. Women's group members are overburdened and have little free time to devote to peace-building. Often, their training is insufficient for organizing peace-building activities. There is virtually no cross-semination of peace-building experiences in southern Sudan, where successes and failures could serve as useful case studies for other women's groups who want to embark on this course. Kinship systems have been replaced by civic organizations that lack female representation. Networking is the buzzword for advocacy but poor infrastructure and fighting curtail possibilities for travel within Sudan.

Aware of how isolation dents women's ability to function in a vibrant way, in June 2000 UNIFEM sponsored a delegation of northern and southern Sudanese women from NGOs and political organizations to New York and Washington, DC, in the United States. This opportunity to promote the concept that women could hasten a just end to the war by having a higher profile in the peace process was invaluable for the chance it gave Sudanese constituencies to mobilize international support. The women met and talked to senior UN officials, US women's and church groups, and human rights activists. This rare exposure to international forums was a unique learning experience that honed the women's advocacy skills and strengthened their resolve to influence policy.[82] The delegation was also awarded a peace prize by the National Peace Foundation in Washington, DC, an accolade that must have gone a long way to boosting the morale of women who had fought long and hard on behalf of their sisters with little outside recognition.

Recognizing that women are an untapped resource for peace, the UN Security Council adopted a resolution in October 2000 that for the first time specifically links women to issues concerning peace and security. Resolution 1325 is seminal to women's struggle for legitimacy in formal peacemaking processes and a seat at negotiating tables. It provides a political framework within which their protection and their role in peace-building can be addressed. The resolution marks a turning point in the evolution of policy by acknowledging that war affects women differently from men; that their protection is neglected; and that their contributions to peace-building have been marginalized. Further, it declares that women and civil organizations should be part of the peacekeeping process and calls for the capacity of women in this role to be built up.

The debate on women, peace and security was revived a year later in October 2001 when women peace leaders spoke of war-induced violence against women to Security Council members, NGO representatives and independent experts. At the same time, female policy-makers called for warring parties and the international community to ensure that women are included in peace processes in a meaningful way.

We have seen that even after several years, women's protection is glaringly neglected in many war-torn countries and that their contributions to peace-building processes are still being marginalized.

Noeleen Heyzer, UNIFEM Executive Director

in a speech to the UN Security Council

Placing women in the peace-building mainstream was the key policy shift that participants in women's affairs from the seven states party to IGAD examined when they attended a UNIFEM-supported seminar in Khartoum. Delegates called for clear links between women's peace initiatives and regional initiatives on peace-building and conflict prevention. They recommended the creation of a broad-based Women's Forum for Peace and Development at regional, subregional and national levels. And they urged that all IGAD policies and programmes pertaining to conflict and peace not only be formulated from the perspective of gender equality but also be sensitive to issues specifically concerning women.

Women have traditionally been looked at as victims but the new thinking is the role that women can play as peacekeepers, in peace accords and the rebuilding of society . . . women tend to listen more so they tend to be more open to the other side's point of view. They also seem to be better at transmitting messages of peace. If a peace accord has been signed, women seem to be good at convincing their spouses and the community that it should be carried out. They also seem to be better at traditional means of negotiation that might work in a community. They are less hierarchical than men. If there is an attempt at a meeting which doesn't come off they tend to go for a second time whereas men tend to be more offended.

IRIN interview with Angela King, UN Secretary-General's Special Adviser on

Gender Issues and Advancement of Women, 31 October 2001

Several women's NGOs operating inside and outside southern Sudan already emphasize peacekeeping and conflict resolution. Donors should tap and expand their resources. The New Sudan Women's Federation, comprising Dinkas and women from Equatoria, is reaching out across the ethnic divide to offer paralegal training to Nuer communities. The Sudan Women's Voice for Peace is in the vanguard of disseminating peace-building skills among women community leaders.

They have built a Peace Demonstration Centre in Mapel that will become a forum for an array of peace-oriented activities including discussions on sexual violence. 'Some of these organizations started by funding themselves. Our commitment as women is as volunteers. We want to be examples to other women,' says Anisia Achieng, who heads SWVP. On the advocacy front, the organization spreads the message of peace through posters and community theatre and by educating its constituents in women's rights. SWVP also assists with income generation as it believes no woman can be a useful agent for peace until she is economically self-sufficient.

SWAN is another organization that emphasizes conflict resolution. It exercises what it terms 'solving disputes' by bringing women together to discuss the common problems that arise from caring for children and extended families, poverty, trauma-tization, illiteracy and marginalization from the decision-making process. Disputes are resolved by discussion between the two parties in the presence of colleagues. During these sessions, the two women who are in dispute are not allowed to leave the room for any reason until they have reached an amicable settlement through dialogue. 'We blame others instead of taking responsibility for what happens to us ourselves. So we deliberately aim dialogue at examining the social process and identifying what role we can play in Sudanese society,' says SWAN chairperson Pauline Riak.

Women are not necessarily more committed than men to the greater good of their communities or less susceptible to partisan agendas. However, the experiences that brought them to peace-building provide an exceptional perspective. Women who end up at the negotiating table generally arrived there by means of civic activism. They also have firsthand experience of the brutal consequences of conflict. They witness vivid links between violence, poverty and inequality in their daily lives. It could be argued that women have a better understanding of the concept that successful peace-building is based on grassroots participation and consensus.[83]

recommendations

* In recognition of women as an untapped resource for peace, all peacemaking organizations and frameworks, governments, UN agencies, NGOs and civil authorities should make every effort to include women and women's organizations in negotiating and implementing peace processes from grassroots to policy-making level.
* It should be acknowledged that exploration for oil exacerbates the conflict. Parties to the conflict should cease all violations of the human rights of civilians, especially the use of helicopter gunships against non-combatants.
* UN agencies and NGOs should underwrite the rehabilitation of infrastructure of abandoned border villages so that inhabitants may return in the wake of the Wunlit Peace Conference.

129

• When a peace settlement has been agreed, UN agencies and NGOs should underwrite the equal provision of services such as water, sanitation, health and education to returnees to hasten their reintegration into society. Infrastructure should include joint schools for Nuer and Dinka children wherever possible.

conclusion

As described in the previous chapters, southern Sudanese women's quality of life is hostage to a patriarchal society that has been disrupted by long-term conflict.

Patriarchal systems are not suited to modern wars waged with efficient weapons of destruction. In Sudan, two-thirds of the adult population are women, many of whom are the single head of household. Under these circumstances, aspects of patriarchy such as forced and early marriages and widow inheritance are neither efficient nor appropriate. Wives do not control their property nor do they have the final say in decisions regarding their children. This has negative implications for women who want to start up businesses and girls who would like to complete their secondary education. Even basic survival is thrown into doubt. Widows who have been inherited by a brother and wives in a polygamous marriage can be penalized in the sharing of resources, including food. This situation calls for adaptation rather than cultural revolution because the collapse of traditional structures, particularly in times of crisis, reduces the ability to cope with the crisis. So the rituals that accompany name-giving, marriage, birth and death should be reinforced.[84] But restrictive customs need to be modified so that women can expand their opportunities as they need and merit.

In times of scarcity, such as war, bridewealth is viewed as brideprice. Daughters become economic bargaining chips that can buy impoverished families survival time. The ramifications are considerable. Early and forced marriages institutionalize female illiteracy, sanction sexual violence and erode women's self-esteem. The solution—women's empowerment—is neither instant nor easy. It lies in greater access to resources such as education and health, rights awareness and protection under the penal code that has been drawn up under the aegis of the Sudan People's Liberation Movement. Donors should support and encourage empowerment initiatives such as the New Sudan Women's Federation training of both women and men to be paralegals. They should also consider funding human rights research pertaining to women. And because men's frustration at being unable to provide for their families is a flashpoint for violence, empowerment should be holistic and include men as well.

Patrilineal inheritance could wreak particularly disastrous consequences for women and children in view of the unchecked spread of HIV. According to customary law, widows and their children cannot inherit property and must rely on the good will of the dead husband's brother for support. If AIDS becomes a scourge, its victims will almost inevitably be stigmatized and the widows and orphans made outcasts. It is vital for their survival that their property is protected through the new penal code.

Seroprevalence has not yet reached the pandemic scale that it has in some other African countries, but it will do so if drastic interventions are not implemented urgently. However, reaching the majority of the population with messages on safe sex practices and other HIV/AIDS information is a daunting proposition. The high rate of illiteracy and the absence of radios and other means of communication means that AIDS education among the adult population has to be delivered on a person-to-person basis. Education of the youth is also a challenge. Less than 15% of children of primary age go to school and many of these, particularly girls, drop out after a few years.[85] On top of that, schools are far flung and often inaccessible because of floods, fighting and lack of transport.

Women have already displayed their adaptability in the realm of shifting gender relations. When war and death rob them of their men, they gamely step into the void, often without benefit of formal education or experienced advice. Given this determination and flexibility, it is logical that women should be included in decision-making on an equal footing with men. They must be party to formulating all aspects of their lives as opposed to involvement in token women's activities. This means positions of influence in water, sanitation, health, education and other sectors of the administration. It means being appointed to the committees of agricultural cooperatives. It means sitting in court as judges and magistrates to safeguard their rights and those of their families. It means equal access to education and an enormous increase in the number of women teachers and head mistresses to foster a new generation of leaders, activists, wives and mothers.

A sound knowledge of democracy and rights is integral to achieving these ends. Independent forms of civic association such as women's groups and community cooperatives have sprung up in most counties. If they are to take root, members need to experience and understand the electoral process—as happened in the Nairobi elections cited in the chapter on women's status in society. A genuine comprehension of democracy will encourage transparency and accountability and promote the interests of the entire group. Likewise, a true understanding of human rights, and particularly women's rights, will not come about until women have a proper sense of their own worth. This is propagated through achievement, recognition and praise.

Women who have stepped into the shoes of their dead or absent husbands are fertile ground for sowing the seeds of empowerment. Yet even they often resist changing their attitudes. Many women cling to their traditional role and become more conservative in times of conflict as they seek the reassuring touchstone of normality. It must never be forgotten that they are traumatized by sexual violence, aerial bombardment and the constant fear of it, abduction, displacement, exile, bereavement of loved ones and atrocities inflicted by weapon-bearing men. Donors need to look at culturally appropriate ways to develop psychosocial programmes that will restore their ability to function properly. This goes hand in hand with bolstering women's self-esteem, which is woefully low inside Sudan and in refugee camps. It is slightly higher in urban settings outside Sudan. There will be no meaningful, practical progress without first addressing the well-being of the ego.

Women need role models, such as schoolteachers, who have shed the stereotype female image of the obedient and passive victim to become independent thinkers with the courage of their own convictions. Literacy and association provide opportunities for this because they allow women to exchange ideas and learn new things. Without this intellectual cross-fertilization there can be no expansion or development. During the course of research for this book, the women's repeated invocation was to end their isolation so that they could build bridges of dialogue among communities, ethnic groups and political factions. This process is a basic building block for peacemaking too. Sitouna Abdalla of the New Sudan Women's Federation suggests that NGOs pool funds to create a radio network for women so that they can communicate with each other more easily.

While workshops and seminars are useful, inevitably they inform only a handful of the population. The argument is strong for assimilating these ideas through hands-on experience. Sudanese cultures put great store by the maxim 'seeing is believing'. To optimize the benefits of workshops and seminars, it is suggested that the large depository of knowledge that resides with urban refugee organizations such as Nairobi's SWAN should be exported back into Sudan. External assistance could be channelled into southern Sudan through these organizations as well. Women from them could conduct training in the local language. Women who use the native idiom carry impact because their audience feels that they are speaking the truth.

Women's organizations that do work in Sudan find it hard to follow up on their training efforts because of the expense of air charter seats and the lack of transport once on the ground. Report writing is another stumbling block. Donors should fund courses on how to write the concepts and budgets for project proposals while at the same time, they should be more flexible in considering proposals that are intrinsically good even if not written in standard form.

If urban refugee women's associations share the lessons they have learned, women's associations inside Sudan can become the lightning rod for democratization and women's rights. This is badly needed. The failure of indigenous women's groups to draw up a cohesive agenda has robbed them of collective bargaining power with their own leaders and with the world beyond. If the women of Yambio, referred to in the chapter on women's status in and out of war zones, had understood that solidarity is a tool, they would not have had to shelve their import business when they ran up against the men's trucking cartel.

And finally on this point, women must be educated on the issues that are central to democracy so that they can cast considered votes on their future as and when a post-ceasefire referendum is held. Regional neighbours have experimented with various permutations of federalism as has Sudan itself in the aftermath of the 1972 Addis Ababa Accord. Political and historical awareness helps people forge meaningful decisions about the future. And whatever the permutation of political solution—federation, confederation, secession or union—none will hold without an educated south that can be an equal partner to the north.

The degree of influence women exert in the public domain is a reflection of their social status. Literate women and those linked to the military and civil structures find it easier to make themselves heard than women who have not been to school or who are self-employed. Unfortunately, the vast majority of women fall into the latter two categories. This means that a large body of innate wisdom is never heard in public forums. This failure to seek out the opinions and thought processes of civic society is particularly marked when both men and women are present. But disregard for the voice of the people occurs in all-women forums as well. The bias towards giving literate women a higher rank is reinforced further by the practice of selecting the same nucleus of women to attend conferences and workshops. Thus a culture of elitism has been unintentionally fostered.

Women's potential for contributing towards peace and development is tremendous as can be seen by their debut forays into these areas through institutions such as women's associations and the New Sudan Council of Churches peace processes and through organizations such as the Sudan Women's Voice for Peace and the New Sudan Women's Federation. Funding for conflict resolution should constitute a far larger part of donor budgets. One option could be to make the disbursement of relief and development budgets conditional to progress in implementing ceasefires and holding fruitful peace negotiations.

If southern Sudanese women are truly to make strides forward, the humanitarian world must reassess its approach to assistance. This means a commitment that extends beyond lifesaving activities to building resiliency and capacity for recovery. This includes promoting self-reliance through income generation, strengthening coping mechanisms, promoting human rights and preparing for peace. Agencies should make sure they plan their programmes in consultation with the communities on the ground when they do this and that women are allowed to air their views fully and freely.

The Operation Lifeline Sudan (OLS) relief operation has been running since 1989, which has led some to say that a decade-long emergency is an oxymoron. Semantics aside, it became patently clear to the researchers for this book that all Sudanese women, no matter what their circumstances, were desperate for development.

In areas where bombing raids are frequent, the rationale for building expensive infrastructure falls away. But there is no reason why women should not be given a step up by providing them with food seeds and low-cost materials to start up small businesses. Donors could benefit tens of thousands of women in regions of conflict by disbursing small grants to women's associations as start-up money for micro enterprise. As the women of Nyal point out in the chapter on women's status in and out of war zones, if they had that, they could feed, clothe and educate their families despite military attack and displacement. At the same time, women should have access to literacy classes and basic accounting. Numeracy is important to dispel mistrust and engender transparency in the collective business dealings of women's groups.

Women in and out of crisis zones would be eligible for this sort of assistance. This includes displaced women and women in refugee camps. Sudanese refugees have been resident at Kakuma in northern Kenya for more than a decade. Even so, official camp policy dictates that while skills can be learned in the camp, they must be put on the back burner until refugees return back home. Why should women who weave beautiful carpets, for instance, not sell them in Nairobi? The contemporary reality is that Kakuma is not a staging point. It is their life. Refugee women should be accorded the dignity of living it as fully as they can.

Agencies and NGOs should also take the long-term view as well as establishing stop-gap means of support for women and their families. Important as micro income-generation projects are, economically marginal activities such as selling tea are no substitute for stimuli of growth such as commerce and trade. Now is the time to lay the foundations for long-term development.

137

The reason for putting some of these suggestions in place is very good. Otherwise, the past will become prologue to another cycle of violence and revenge that cuts a swathe of devastation through civil society. No effort is too great to prevent this from happening as all women from southern Sudan will tell you. Ask any one of them to voice her greatest hope and she will reply—peace.

notes

[1] Nilima Chawla, *Survival to Thrival: Children and Women in the Southern Part of Sudan* (Nairobi: UNICEF [no date]); SPLM Health Commission position paper on HIV/AIDS in the New Sudan (October 2000); SCF, CARE International and Oxfam paper, 'Sudan: Who Has the Will for Peace?' (22 October 1998).

[2] Anthony Wangi, 'Women, Girls and Children Are the Hardest Hit in the Raging War', *The Women Today* (publication of New Sudan Women Federation) no. 18 (July–August 2000).

[3] 'Christians' Plight in Sudan Tests a Bush Stance', Washington Post (24 March 2001).

[4] Amnesty International, 'Sudan: The Human Price of Oil', report (May 2000).

[5] Address report to UN General Assembly, 8 November 2001.

[6] Amnesty, 'Human Price of Oil'.

[7] Leonardo Franco, UN Special Rapporteur to the Sudan.

[8] Christian Aid, 'The Scorched Earth: Oil and War in Sudan', eyewitness report, 15 March 2001.

[9] ibid.

[10] Amnesty, 'Human Price of Oil'.

[11] Amnesty, 'Human Price of Oil'.

[12] UN Office for Coordination of Humanitarian Affairs Integrated Regional Information Network (IRIN), 'Relief Workers Say Helicopter Fired on Fleeing Civilians' (27 February 2002) and 'Oil-related Clashes in Western Upper Nile' (28 February 2002).

[13] US Committee for Refugees Annual Report 2001.

[14] Sudanese Women's Association in Nairobi (SWAN), presen-tation paper to Mr Gaim Kebreab, NCA Regional Representative for East Africa (30 September 1999).

[15] UNICEF, 'Education for All', assessment report on southern Sudan (April 2001).

[16] New Sudan Women's Federation, 'Overcoming Gender Conflict and Bias: The Case of New Sudan Women and Girls' (Nairobi: Jacaranda Designs, 2001).

[17] Simon Harragin with Chol Changath Chol, 'The Southern Sudan Vulnerability Study' (Save the Children Fund (UK), 17 June 1998).

[18] Resolution no. 16, SPLM/SPLA National Convention 1994.

[19] Suzanne Jambo, speech at the launch of the NSWF gender book, 31 October 2001.

[20] Report of the Judicial Committee, 'Woman and Child Rights in the Context of the Legal System and the Judicial Structures of the New Sudan', August 2000.

[21] ibid.

[22] ibid.

[23] Customary law in Nuer States of Upper Nile and Jonglei, in Leech State, Western Upper Nile; restatement of Bahr el Ghazal Region Customary Law (Amended) Act 1984, Bahr el Ghazal Region Act No. 1, 1984.

[24] Jane A. Andanje, 'Gender Analysis in Complex Emergencies: The Case of Southern Sudan', gender and development dissertation (Institute of Development Studies, University of Sussex, September 2000).

[25] UNICEF, 'Education for All'; Save the Children, CARE International and Oxfam (GB), 'Who Has the Will for Peace?', report (22 October 1998).

[26] Brian Edeba, 'Reviving Education: An Uphill Task', *Africanews* (issue 69, December 2001).

[27] ibid.

[28] UNICEF, 'Education for All'.

[29] Elizabeth Otieno, head of Education, New Sudan Council of Churches, Nairobi, Kenya, interview.

[30] Dr Margaret Itto, health coordinator, New Sudan Council of Churches, Nairobi.

[31] Harragin, 'Southern Sudan Vulnerability Study'.

[32] Health service reports collated for the SPLM strategic planning

workshop (New Sudan, 1999); position paper on HIV/AIDS in the New Sudan (SPLM Health Commission, October 2000).

[33] Chawla, *From Survival to Thrival*.

[34] Personal interviews with Sudanese women in Dadaab Camp, Kenya; New Sudan Women's Federation, 'Overcoming Gender Conflict and Bias'.

[35] Chawla, *From Survival to Thrival*.

[36] Jok Madut Jok, *Militarism, Gender and Reproductive Suffering: The Case of Abortion in Western Dinka* (Los Angeles: Loyola Marymount University, Dept. of History [no date]).

[37] Chawla, *From Survival to Thrival*.

[38] ibid.

[39] Letter from Nicholas Siwingwa, World Food Programme deputy country director, Sudan, to Alastair Lyon, Reuters bureau chief, Cairo, February 2001.

[40] Jok, *Militarism, Gender and Reproductive Suffering*, chap. 10, 'War, Kinship and Gender Relations'.

[41] UNHCR fact sheet: 'Refugees by Numbers 2001'.

[42] Personal interview with women at Kakuma refugee camp.

[43] Statute of Office of the United Nations High Commissioner for Refugees, General Assembly Resolution 428 (V) of 14 December 1950, Art. 8 (c).

[44] Correspondence with Barbara E. Harrell-Bond, distinguished visiting professor, Forced Migration and Refugee Studies, American University in Cairo; 'Regional Refugee Trends Update' (Refugee Consortium of Kenya, October 2000); Guglielmo Verdirame, 'Refugees in Kenya: Between a Rock and a Hard Place' (Refugee Studies Programme, Oxford University, 1997); interview with James Miriti, legal officer, Refugee Consortium of Kenya, Nairobi.

[45] Interview by Mary Anne Fitzgerald with women at Elit Camp, Haikota, Eritrea, May 2000.

[46] Interviews with Pauline Riak, executive director of SWAN, Nairobi, and Sitouna Abdalla, chairwoman of New Sudan Women's Federation,

Nairobi.

[47] New Sudan Women's Federation, 'Overcoming Gender Conflict and Bias'.

[48] Jok, *Militarism, Gender and Reproductive Suffering*.

[49] Report by Ambrose Riny Thiik, chief justice, the New Sudan, and chairman of the Judicial Committee, 'Woman and Child Rights' (August 2000).

[50] New Sudan Women's Federation, 'Overcoming Gender Conflict and Bias'.

[51] Personal interview, October 2001.

[52] Andanje, 'Gender Analysis in Complex Emergencies'.

[53] Jok Madut Jok, *Militarization and Gender Violence in South Sudan* (Los Angeles: Loyola Marymount University, Dept. of History [no date]).

[54] Anna Kima, NSCC peace mobilizer; field research for UNIFEM by Atsango Chesoni.

[55] Jok, *Militarism, Gender and Reproductive Suffering*.

[56] Jok, *Militarization and Gender Violence in South Sudan*.

[57] Customary laws in Leech State (Western Upper Nile).

[58] New Sudan Women's Federation, 'Overcoming Gender Conflict and Bias'.

[59] Dengtiel A. Kur, 'The Impact of War on Children and the Role of Traditional Values and International Humanitarian Principles in South Sudan', research carried out jointly by the South Sudan Law Society and Larjour Consultancy in the rebel-held areas of southern Sudan (compiled for South Sudan Law Society, June 1996); includes section by Dr Simon Simonse, 'Children, Values and War in South Sudan' covering research carried out in the context of the Graça Machel study in the East Bank of Equatoria.

[60] Harragin, 'Southern Sudan Vulnerability Study'.

[61] Sharon Elaine Hutchinson, 'Sacrificing Childhood: the Impact of Sudan's Unresolved Civil War on the Lives of Nuer and Dinka Women and Children', Development of Strategic Objectives Phase 2 (Save the Children Denmark, May 1998–April 1999)

[62] Information from Julianna Lindsey on a UNICEF proposal.

[63] UNDP, 'Southern Sudan HIV/AIDS/STD Situation Analysis, December 1997–January 1998'.

[64] ibid.

[65] ibid.; SPLM Health Commission, 'Position Paper on HIV/AIDS in the New Sudan, October 2000', draft no. 5: 22/01/01.

[66] American Refugee Council as told to Dr Margaret Itto, NSCC.

[67] *Washington Notes on Africa*, vol. 26 (Spring 2000): special issue, 'Slavery, War and Peace in Sudan', an updated briefing paper (Washington, DC : Washington Office on Africa).

[68] United Nations Commission on Human Rights, Sub-Commission on the Promotion and Protection of Human Rights, Working Group on Contemporary Forms of Slavery, 25th Session, Geneva, 14–23 June 2000.

[69] Interview with Jane S.P. Mocellin, senior consultant, Psychosocial Preparedness and Response in Disasters and Emergencies Capacity Building Training and Programming, WHO.

[70] Heather Stewart, Trackmark managing director, Lokichoggio, Kenya, who flew the survivors out of Sudan for medical treatment.

[71] Interviews with Mocellin and Sudanese women counsellors.

[72] *We Have to Sit Down: Women, War and Peace in Southern Sudan* (Pax Christi, 1998).

[73] Julianne Duncan, 'Best-Interest Assessment Interviews: Summary of Findings and Recommendations', for Kakuma refugee camp, Kenya (UNHCR, January 2000); Jane S.P. Mocellin, UNICEF senior consultant, 'Psychosocial Support in War-Torn Southern Sudan: Needs Assessment Report', prepared for UNICEF/OLS Education Section and Protection Section, Nairobi and Geneva, 30 June 2000.

[74] Kiki van Kessel, 'No Time for Childhood: Psychosocial Interventions for Children in War-torn Sudan', master's thesis, Department of Development Studies, Catholic University of Nijmegen, 1996; Mocellin, 'Psychosocial Support'; Duncan, 'Best-Interest Assessment Interviews'.

[75] Julianne Duncan, 'Overview of Mental Health Findings for UAM

[Unaccompanied Minors] and Separated Children Interviewed as Part of UNHCR Best-Interest Determinations', Kakuma refugee camp, Kakuma, Kenya, 20 January 2000.

[76] Mocellin, 'Psychosocial Support'.

[77] ibid.

[78] Mary Y. Okumu, 'Bringing Beijing Home: In Search of More Relevant Ways of Combating Violence against Women in Africa', El-Taller Africa.

[79] Mocellin, 'Psychosocial Support'.

[80] *Customary Law for the Nuer States of Upper Nile and Jonglei*; chapter 1, Murder; Article 3, Sectional Fighting.

[81] Christian Aid, 'The Scorched Earth'.

[82] Narrative and financial report for Women in Search of a Just Peace in Sudan: a Sudanese women's advocacy mission to the USA; reporting period 1 May–31 July 2000.

[83] Support to Sudanese Women's Empowerment for Peace, project document (Royal Netherlands Embassy, Nairobi, Kenya, and Khartoum, Sudan, December 2000).

[84] *We Have to Sit Down*.

[85] UNICEF, 'Education for All'.